Macmillan International College Editions (MICE) will bring to university, college, school and professional students, authoritative paperback books covering the history and cultures of the developing world, and the special aspects of its scientific, medical, technical, social and economic development. The MICE programme contains many distinguished series in a wide range of disciplines, some titles being regionally biassed, others being more international. Library editions will usually be published simultaneously with the paperback editions. For full details of this list, please contact the publishers.

Other titles of interest
General Editor Professor A. N. Jeffares
Commonwealth Writers Series
Robson: *Ngugi wa Thiong'o*
Carroll: *Chinua Achebe*
Kiernan: *Patrick White*
Gurr and Hanson: *Katherine Mansfield*

New Literature Handbooks
King: *West Indian Literature*
King: *The New English Literatures – cultural nationalism in a changing world*

Rutherford and Hannah: *Commonwealth Short Stories*
Burton and Chacksfield: *African Poetry in English*
Larson: *The Emergence of African Fiction*

BACKGROUND TO SHAKESPEARE

M. M. Badawi
Fellow of St Antony's College,
Oxford

MACMILLAN
EDUCATION

First published 1981
Reprinted 1986, 1987

Published by
MACMILLAN EDUCATION LTD
Houndmills, Basingstoke, Hampshire RG21 2XS
and London
Companies and representatives
throughout the world

Printed in Hong Kong

ISBN 0–333–30535–3

Contents

FOR MIEKE

Preface

This book is designed primarily for the overseas student of Shakespeare, especially for the Afro-Asian student with no classical and little or no Christian background. That is why it attempts to take very little for granted. The assumptions which lie behind the works of Shakespeare, and for that matter behind the whole body of Western literature, and that are tacitly accepted by the English and the European reader are here explicitly stated in order to provide the reader with the frame of reference necessary for the understanding and appreciation of Shakespeare's plays. Similarly, the language of exposition is deliberately made straightforward and complex issues are presented in a manner which may at times border on simplification. However, I have endeavoured not to lose sight of my specific reader, and if by the end of the book he feels that he has been helped in understanding Shakespearean drama or that at least some obstacles have been removed from his path, my labour will not have been in vain. In short, I have tried to write the kind of book which I wished I had read on my first introduction to English literature.

It is hoped that, beside being a useful introduction when it is read straight through from beginning to end, the book may prove to be of some value to the student as a work of reference. With this latter end in mind I have provided a comprehensive index.

Finally, I should like to express my gratitude to my friend Professor Mahmoud Manzalaoui, of the University of British Columbia, who kindly read the first draft of this book and made many valuable suggestions.

St Antony's College, Oxford   M. M. Badawi

The Swan Theatre: a sketch made in 1596.

1 The Study of Shakespeare

At the outset an attempt should be made to define what is meant by the study of Shakespeare. Surely, we could imagine some one saying, a Shakespearean play, like any other work of art, is simply something to be read and enjoyed. Why then, our imaginary person might go on, do we need to 'study' Shakespeare? Our answer to such a question would be something like this: indeed a Shakespearean play is to be read, acted and enjoyed; however, for proper enjoyment it must first be understood, since it is only too easy to enjoy a work of art for the wrong reasons.

A number of things stand in the way of understanding Shakespeare. In the first place we are not always sure that what we are reading is Shakespeare himself. I do not mean that we do not know for certain the identity of the author, whether it was William Shakespeare or some one else, say the Earl of Oxford or Francis Bacon, who wrote the plays generally ascribed to Shakespeare. I do not think it matters much who wrote them provided we know that they were all written by the same man. I say 'all' because, although each play is a separate and individual work of art, they all generally illuminate one another, and taken together they form an impressive achievement in which each individual play acquires more weight and dignity when placed against the background of the whole corpus. Each play is more or less a landmark in the road along which Shakespeare the artist travelled, or, to change the metaphor, each play is a variation on a number of themes that recur in the poet's work. It is a good idea to settle this question of the authorship of the plays here and to point out its exact significance or rather insignificance, because much ink has been spilled over it. Besides, at first the overseas student often tends to busy himself with such biographical irrelevancies. This is because of the difficulties he encounters in understanding the text of a poet who, he is told time and again, is perhaps the greatest single figure in modern literature. In this connection we may do well to remember the words of T. S. Eliot in his famous essay 'Tradition and individual talent', 'To divert interest from the poet to the poetry is a laudable aim'.

It is not, therefore, the uncertainty as to the authorship of the Shakespearean canon that is meant, but our uncertainty as regards the authenticity of the complete text of the individual plays, which we know, or at least assume, to be the work of Shakespeare. Shakespeare's plays, like many old texts, present peculiar problems which do not arise in the case of the works of a modern dramatist. Shakespeare did not prepare his plays for the press himself. Unlike his contemporary Ben Jonson, Shakespeare did not publish his complete works in his life time. The first collected edition of his works, which contained all the plays except *Pericles* but none of the poems, appeared in 1623 seven years after his death. This is the book known as the First Folio, and it was prepared for the press by his sometime fellow actors John Heminges and Henry Condell. Because Shakespeare did not supervise its printing it was natural to believe that it contained many errors, especially when we remember the printing methods of the time, and even assuming that the Folio was printed from the author's own manuscript. If you compare the First Folio with any of the modern standard editions of Shakespeare, for example, the Globe Edition, you will find a number of textual differences ranging from variation in the reading of a single word to the presence or absence of whole scenes.

How then, did this situation arise? No edition of Shakespeare's complete works appeared in his life time, and it would therefore seem reasonable to regard the First Folio as the authoritative text of the plays. Unfortunately the matter is slightly complicated because a number of individual plays were published many years before the First Folio. These individual plays are known as the Quartos. It soon became clear to scholars that the text of a play in the Folio differs, considerably at times, from that of the Quarto. Since the Quartos as a rule are older than the First Folio, scholars who wanted to arrive as near as possible to a perfect text felt the need to collate or compare the various Quartos with the Folio, especially when they came across an obscure passage which did not easily make sense. A further complication arose as a result of the discovery that not all the Quartos are equally 'good' or reliable. Although such scholars, known as editors, have been working on Shakespeare's text since the beginning of the eighteenth century, there are still certain passages in which it cannot be said that we have Shakespeare's own words. In a handbook of this size, which attempts to cover such a wide field, it is clearly impossible to relate the story of the text of the plays or to trace, however briefly, the various stages through which it passed before it reached its present, generally accepted form. But we have to include a word about the text here, since if we want to understand Shakespeare we must make sure that we have his own words and nobody else's. Therefore, it matters a great deal which particular edition of his plays we read—a fact which tends to puzzle many students. However, when a student is reminded that Shakespeare was primarily a dramatist writing in verse, a medium in which the individual word or image sometimes counts (as close verbal analysis can often show us) and when he is given an idea of the background against which the text of the plays originated, the source of bewilderment often disappears. Luckily the task of editing Shakespeare, that is, of preparing a reliable text for the reader, is so highly specialised and needs such a severe technical training in Elizabethan orthography (spelling) and calligraphy (handwriting) as well as such a vast amount of reading in contemporary literature, that no beginner need, or even can, concern himself with it. It is enough for him to realise that this constitutes one branch of the study of Shakespeare, in many ways the most indispensable, and we must be grateful that there are people who spend many years of their lives labouring to provide us with a reasonably perfect text of Shakespeare's plays.

Another source of difficulty in understanding Shakespeare is the different background of the plays, their social, political, but more especially intellectual and artistic background. It is true that Shakespeare is one of the most universal of all writers. Still he is a poet and poetry, especially great poetry, is at once most local and most universal. When a poet is as great as Shakespeare he uses language at its highest potency and, unlike other artistic media, words are the storehouse of the experiences of a whole people. It is only through the transmutation of what is local and national that a poet attains universality. Poetic language is never an abstract language. On the contrary, it is often, and in Shakespeare's case it is nearly always, full of concrete imagery. Quite often the full force of an image can only be felt in its natural and immediate context, sometimes in the purely physical or geographical sense of the word. A student familiar with the geography of England will get more out of Shakespeare's nature imagery than one whose experience does not go beyond a desert landscape, or who has only seen evergreen trees. This is platitudinous, but needs to be affirmed. What may be less obvious is that the context of what seems to be a familiar image may vary from one age to another. Take a simple example, like the word 'hangman'. In *Macbeth* after murdering King Duncan Macbeth, almost demented, staggers back to his wife to tell her, among other things, of the prayers he has just heard the king's two sons utter in their sleep:

> One cried, 'God bless us!' and, 'Amen', the other,
> As they had seen me with these hangman's hands.
>   (II ii 26–27)

The full force of the image here would certainly be missed even by a modern Englishman unless he was told that often the job of a hangman in Shakespeare's time did not end at hanging criminals, but he also had to draw (disembowel) and quarter them. Seen in this context the image reveals how drenched in blood Macbeth's imagination was. It is no wonder then that he thought that his hands would turn the colour of the whole ocean red.

Related to this is the obvious need to know Elizabethan English. It is a well known fact that like all living things language is subject to the law of change. In Elizabethan times some words had certain meanings or shades of meaning which they subsequently lost. For instance, in *Hamlet* the full implication of the Prince's words to Ophelia 'Get thee to a nunnery' (III i) would not be appreciated unless we knew that the word 'nunnery' was also Elizabethan cant for 'brothel'. Likewise, when Hamlet tells Polonius (II ii) that he knows that he is a 'fishmonger' he is not simply talking nonsense in an attempt to lead Polonius to believe that he is mad, or hinting at the fact that Polonius is trying to 'fish out' his secret from him. He is also alluding to the disgraceful way Polonius is using his daughter as a bait for Hamlet, for to an Elizabethan audience 'fishmonger' suggested 'a procurer of women'. Needless to say this multiplicity of meaning which contributes to the rich texture of Shakespeare's verse could not be seen without a thorough knowledge of the Elizabethan idiom.

What is even more relevant is that Shakespeare was a dramatist, and drama, perhaps more than any other art form, has to have an immediate appeal. Again the question of Shakespeare's universality has to be explained here. Shakespeare's plays are not moral or philosophical treatises on man, but are works originally written to be produced on a particular stage to satisfy the taste of a particular audience. Shakespeare was a successful dramatist and no dramatist could possibly succeed unless he spoke the same language as his audience, unless he presented matters in terms they could understand. Shakespeare's universality is expressed in terms of his time and place. His heroes, it has been claimed, are not Roman or Greek or Italian, but are essentially human beings. In his *Preface to Shakespeare* (1765) Dr Johnson says, 'His story requires Romans or kings, but he thinks only on men'. True enough, but they are men behaving and thinking like Elizabethan Englishmen. It is, therefore, imperative to know something about the ways the Elizabethans behaved and what they thought about matters of life and death in order to be able to see the problems Shakespeare posed in his plays in their true proportions. The slightest shift of emphasis can lead to distortions and false interpretations. Examples of such false interpretations are numerous, even within the Western tradition itself. The problem of Hamlet was distorted by the German poet Goethe. In Victorian England Helena in *All's Well That Ends Well* was falsely accused of immodestly chasing an unwilling young man, and in twentieth century England Isabella in *Measure for Measure* was equally falsely accused of being cold and unfeeling. We have even been told by a modern English critic that Shakespeare meant us to believe that Romeo's duty was clearly not to avenge Mercutio's death, and that Hamlet was wrong in listening to the ghost and in trying to avenge his father's murder. This is to attribute to Shakespeare ideas which do not reasonably seem to be his own and consequently to miss his universality in the long run. To be able to see this universality in its proper perspective one has first to see the problems of his heroes and heroines in their true nature and proportions. In order to perceive what in his works belongs to all time one must first detect what belongs to his time.

Shakespeare's time had a set of assumptions about man, his

psychological make up, his relation to other men, to the state and the ruler and to God. This we must try to understand, and by a process of sympathetic imagination endeavour to relive the experience of his characters, try to see what life looked like through their eyes and then relate their experiences and problems to our own. For instance, nothing seems more remote from our modern life than the politics of Shakespeare's history plays. Yet when we understand the Elizabethan conception of human history and their own recent history we shall see that the concern of the Elizabethans with history and politics, as is reflected in Shakespeare's plays, was no more passionate or less justifiable than our present concern with problems of communism and capitalism and the question of the relation between the individual and the state. But to perceive this universal relevance of Shakespeare we must first relate him to his time. Hence we have another branch of the study of Shakespeare, which consists of attempts to find out the truth about the social and intellectual life of Shakespeare's England. Such attempts are motivated not so much by historical or archaeological curiosity as by a desire to arrive at a fuller understanding of the poet's works. We must also be careful not to apply our knowledge of the background in a mechanical or simplistic fashion. *The Elizabethan World Picture* made famous by the scholar E. M. W. Tillyard (Chatto and Windus, London, 1943) is not necessarily and in all its details the world picture of Shakespeare or even of all his characters.

One particular aspect of this background deserves to be mentioned separately because of its crucial importance, namely the Elizabethan stage conditions. Shakespeare, we have said, was primarily a dramatist writing for a particular stage. It is, therefore, vitally important to know something about that stage, since this may shed light on the form and structure of his plays. All drama is based upon a set of conventions, so we must ask, 'What are the conventions of Elizabethan drama which Shakespeare had to follow?' If our own stage conditions happen to be different from those of the Elizabethans our task then will be, first, to try not to think in their terms while perusing or acting Shakespeare's plays and, secondly, to reconstruct in our imagination the conditions for which they were written. If, on the other hand, drama is not one of our traditional art forms, since, as T. S. Eliot says, 'the theatre is a gift which has not been vouchsafed to every race, even of the highest culture', the problem is at once made simpler and more difficult. We shall be spared the first task of relinquishing our dramatic habits, but then our second task becomes doubly difficult. We shall have to imagine these plays performed on a stage the best way we can. The task is exceedingly difficult, but by no means impossible. There are few human beings in whom the sense of drama, the tragic or comic sense, cannot be developed. One of the worst things we could do to Shakespeare's plays, however, is to treat them as mere literary exercises, or to read them as if they were novels.

Beside tne study of the text and the study of the social, political, intellectual and artistic background there is another branch of Shakespearean study which aims at a fuller understanding and hence greater enjoyment of the plays. This is the study of the plays. But here someone may ask, 'What is the value of such a that is, a study of the genesis of the plays, of the process of their creation. Such were the Elizabethan stage conditions that there was hot competition among the various theatrical companies in London, and to satisfy the incessantly growing demand of the public dramatists had to work at top speed. The result was that few Elizabethan dramatists, Shakespeare not excluded, invented the stories of their plays. Luckily, in the case of Shakespeare scholars have been able to locate the sources of practically all of his plays. But here someone may ask, 'What is the value of such a study? Is it not enough to study the plays themselves?' This is indeed a valid question, since in the plays themselves we have all that Shakespeare intended to say. However, the study of the source of a Shakespearean play often sheds a good deal of light on Shakespeare's intention. It is true that whatever he borrows from his sources is nearly always transmuted by him in such a way that it becomes an integral part of the general fabric of his plays, it never remains quite the same. However, Shakespeare does not always follow his source and quite often he deliberately deviates from it. Sometimes he even rejects some probability in it in favour of some apparently gross improbability of his own as, for instance, in the case of *Othello*. Now Shakespeare with his celebrated insight into human nature is no fool. He would not commit such an apparent error of judgment without some good reason. It is our duty to ask ourselves whenever Shakespeare seems on purpose to depart from his source why he does so. In trying to find reasonable answers to our questions we obtain more insight into his art.

This brings us to the aesthetic study of the plays themselves. The plays should always be our final destination, all other studies being only tributaries to this. We must never allow ourselves to be tempted to lose sight of the plays while pursuing such studies, any more than we should let A. C. Bradley's book *Shakespearean Tragedy* (Macmillan, London, 1904) replace Shakespeare's plays, a thing which a student is often tempted to do, because reading and understanding the plays themselves is a much more difficult and exacting task. However, once the background of the plays has been explained half the difficulty is removed and we must now concentrate on the study of each individual play. There are various angles from which we can undertake such a study, the most common of which is to approach the play by way of character. Shakespeare's amazing power of characterisation has been the subject of critical commentary ever since the beginning of Shakespearean criticism and it is perhaps his insight into human nature and his ability to create life-like and convincing individuals that first strike a beginner. Since this aspect of Shakespearean drama is the one that can most easily be appreciated let the reader then start by studying it, provided he does not forget that, however life-like it may be, a Shakespearean dramatic character is not to be equated with, or treated as, a real flesh and blood human being. A Shakespearean character is ultimately part of a work of art, it is only a part of a significant pattern from which alone it derives its life and meaning. The reality of Hamlet's predicament, of his fears and doubts, sorrows and ruthless self exploration should indeed be appreciated, but Hamlet himself ought not to be taken out of Shakespeare's Denmark to be psycho-analysed. As a dramatic creation Hamlet is one of Shakespeare's most eloquent characters, but he is a dumb patient, alas!

Since a Shakespearean character is only one part of a total pattern, the rest of this pattern has an equal claim on our attention. It includes plot or structure, poetry, comprising imagery and rhythm as well as the general 'meaning' or significance of the whole pattern, the vision of life expressed in it, the main theme or themes of which each play is an embodiment.

The plot of a play, the arrangement of incidents, their parallelism or juxtaposition, the tempo of their movement and all the other aspects of structure have to be studied, but not in isolation from character and the other constituent parts of the play. Taken in isolation the plot of *Hamlet*, for instance, seems a sprawling, slow and chaotic sequence of events, but, when related to the character of Hamlet and his mode of treating the problem he was forced to face, it becomes clearly a reflection of his inaction. Criticism of a plot which does not attempt to relate it to the other constituent elements of drama can only be superficial and sterile. In the history of Shakespearean criticism there are many examples of such criticism. One of these examples is the type of criticism of plot, so common in the late seventeenth and most of the eighteenth century, which relied upon the mechanical application to Shakespeare's plays of the so-called Aristotelian unities: the unity of place (that is, the action of a play should occur only in one locality); the unity of time (that is, the time of the action represented should not exceed a single revolution of the sun) and the unity of action (that is, a play should deal only with one action). It was a common practice then to analyse the events of Shakespeare's plays with reference to these unities and to show how grossly Shakespeare violates them. Such criticism is as futile as it is childishly easy; it does not tell us much about the plays. On the other hand, a student would learn a lot if he asked himself the reason why Shakespeare changes his scenes so often in a play like *Antony and Cleopatra* or why there are remarkably few changes of scenes in *Othello* once the action has been moved to Cyprus. He would then find that in the former play such changes help expand the setting of the action and contribute towards the global or universal effect of the events and that such changes secure the same effect as that of the dominant type of imagery peculiar to this play. In *Othello*, on the other hand, the dominant effect is one of confinement rather than of liberation. To this effect the infrequent changes of scenes contribute no small part. Again this accords with the obvious theme of the play, which is the trapping of one human being by another, and with the imagery of animals ensnaring one another. Likewise, instead of complaining that there is more than one action in, for instance, *King Lear* the student should more profitably try to see if there is any relation between the main plot (the story of Lear and his daughters) and the sub-plot (the story of Gloucester and his sons). Quite often in Shakespeare the sub-plot is an echo of, or runs parallel to, the main plot thus both enhancing and universalising its effect (as in the case of *King Lear*). In some cases by means of contrast it sets off the main plot (as in the case of *Much Ado About Nothing* where the story of Hero and Claudio is sharply contrasted with that of Benedick and Beatrice). In the comedies realism and romance are not indiscriminately mixed together, but usually scenes of realism and scenes of romance act and react upon one another. The student then should ask himself about the precise nature of the relationship, if there is any, between them. Similarly if in a tragedy a comic scene follows close upon a tragic one the student should try to find out if there is any valid dramatic reason for this, other than the mere desire of the dramatist to provide comic relief. Here the famous example of the porter scene in *Macbeth* comes readily to our minds. Critics have pointed out the subtle and grim ironic relation which this scene bears to the preceding scene of the murder of Duncan, to say nothing of the purely practical purpose it serves in giving Macbeth and Lady Macbeth time to wash and change into their night gowns. Another important part of plot or structure which the student should study in detail is the first scenes of a Shakespearean play. Coleridge was one of the first critics to show us how important they generally are for the purpose of understanding the rest of the play. These are only a few aspects, chosen at random, of useful criticism of plot.

Shakespearean drama is poetic drama. This is a fact to be kept in mind constantly. Now the difference between poetic and prose drama is not simply that the former is written in verse. Great poetic drama, like Shakespeare's, expresses an experience beyond the reach of prose, an experience that touches the deeper layers of the mind. This it does by means of the rich resources of poetry, by means of rhythm, music, semantic complexities and imagery. Hence the importance of the study of Shakespearean music and imagery. A study of one of Shakespeare's great tragedies which deals exclusively with character and plot leaving out the poetry, however penetrating and admirable it may be, is of necessity incomplete. Rhythm affects us in strange ways which are by no means easy to account for, or even to be aware of. And for the overseas student this unfortunately constitutes the most difficult aspect of Shakespearean drama to appreciate. However, we must try and we can, by a conscious effort, train our ears to catch at least something of the subtleties of Shakespearean music. Let me mention here one or two obvious examples. Othello tells

Iago after the latter has robbed him of his peace of mind by sowing the seeds of jealousy in his soul:

> By the world,
> I think my wife be honest, and think she is not;
> I think that thou art just, and think thou art not;
>
> (*Othello* III iii 383–385)

Surely the see-saw rhythm of these two lines expresses most eloquently the state of utter bewilderment and confusion in which Othello's mind is labouring at this moment, not knowing what to believe and what not to believe, whom to trust and whom not to trust. An equally obvious example of a masterly use of rhythm can be found in Macbeth's famous soliloquy in which he utters his thoughts on receiving the news of his wife's death.

> To-morrow, and to-morrow, and to-morrow,
> Creeps in this petty pace from day to day,
> To the last syllable of recorded time;
>
> (*Macbeth* V v 19–21)

Here also it is clear that the first line, broken three times by a short pause following the falling rhythm of 'to-morrow' in each case, magnificently expresses Macbeth's despair and broken spirit. To see this the student only has to compare the broken rhythm here with the easy flowing rhythm of the opening line of the scene, addressed to the soldiers:

> Hang out our banners on the outward walls;

which has the obvious imprint of a sure and confident command.

The study of imagery presents fewer difficulties. A cursory reading of Shakespeare will show us how strikingly figurative his language is. But the student must realise how 'peculiarly organic and vital' his style is, as Coleridge once said. In it one metaphor is developed 'by unmarked influences of association from some preceding metaphor' with the result that his imagery seems to be closely tied together by the most subtle bonds. The soliloquy of Macbeth, from which we have just quoted, is a good enough example to illustrate Shakespeare's amazing power of thinking in images. Macbeth has just received the news of the death of his wife, at whose instigation he committed the murder of Duncan — the murder which altered the whole course of his life, even though it brought him nearer the crown of Scotland. It is thus a fitting moment for him to take stock of his own life, to evaluate what he has achieved (and what she helped him to achieve).

> She should have died hereafter;
> There would have been a time for such a word.
> To-morrow, and to-morrow, and to-morrow,
> Creeps in this petty pace from day to day,
> To the last syllable of recorded time;
> And all our yesterdays have lighted fools
> The way to dusty death'. Out, out, brief candle!
> Life's but a walking shadow, a poor player
> That struts and frets his hour upon the stage,
> And then is heard no more: it is a tale
> Told by an idiot, full of sound and fury,
> Signifying nothing.   (V v 17–28)

There is no general agreement on the meaning of the opening sentence: it may mean either that 'she was bound to die sometime', or that 'she should not have died at this precise moment but later, at a more peaceful time'. Whatever interpretation we may put on this line, the important thing for our purpose is that the present crisis drives Macbeth to think of the future, his future, his 'to-morrows' which have no meaning for him now, but simply creep on until the end of his hopeless life. The 'last syllable' is suggested by the word 'word'. 'Yesterdays' is suggested by 'to-morrow' and probably also by the sound of 'to day'. The 'candle', suggested by 'lighted' in the preceding line, itself suggests 'shadow' and 'shadow' what is unreal and the 'poor player'. The 'player', in turn, suggests the 'tale' full of sound and fury and the 'idiot' hearkens back to the 'fools'. The speech is so organically conceived that one image is related to another by an unconscious or half-conscious process of association, and the whole is a most precise poetic statement of Macbeth's vision of his own life and of life in general at that moment. What the reader will immediately observe is that Macbeth's utter disillusion and despair are revealed by him in terms of images. The title bestowed upon him by Duncan in the beginning of the play, which he thought would bring him nearer the crown (since it showed the truthfulness of the witches who had prophesied the crown for him) was conceived by him as a happy 'prologue' to the 'swelling act of the imperial theme' (I iii 8–9). Now looking back upon his life he finds that 'the imperial theme' on which he has staked the whole of his life has proved nothing but an insignificant tale told by an idiot, a short hour of strutting and fretting upon the stage of unreality. Instead of simply saying that he has wasted his life, or that the whole thing has not been worth all that trouble, Macbeth sees his tragedy, and states it, in the form of a sustained stage metaphor.

Like character or plot, imagery in a Shakespearean play can be most fruitfully studied when related to the rest of the play. In the thirties there appeared a tendency to regard a Shakespearean play as an expanded metaphor and since then a number of studies have been published dealing predominantly with Shakespeare's imagery. Such studies have yielded some extremely interesting results, not the least of which is the discovery that in each play there is often a group of dominant images which reflect its main theme or themes, for instance: the dominant images of disease in *Hamlet*; of light in *Romeo and Juliet*; of wild beasts preying upon one another reflecting the law of the jungle operating in the world of *King Lear* etc. Criticism of imagery has also revealed Shakespeare's symbolical use of certain images, like those of sleep, storm and music. These are indeed valuable and illuminating results. But some of these studies are marred either by their concentration on imagery in isolation and without reference to its immediate context or by the impression they give that there is nothing but imagery in Shakespearean drama and that the student would be wasting his time if he paid some of his attention to other aspects of the plays, such as, for instance, characters.

By a careful analysis of character, plot and imagery, an analysis in which even the results of the fashionable science of linguistics could be used, a student should try to arrive at the main theme or themes of a Shakespearean play. The theme may be the tragic or comic implications of the discrepancy between appearance and reality (*Macbeth, Twelfth Night*); or it may be the conflict between what Sir Philip Sidney calls man's 'erected wit' and his 'infected will'; the conflict between knowledge and will power (*Hamlet*); or between reason and passion (*Othello, Hamlet*). It may be a comment of lasting significance upon the human condition, such as the enormity of human deception (*Othello*); or of human ignorance and the defeat of intellect (*Hamlet*); or the inadequacy of political or social values such as honour (*Henry IV*); or of an abstract ideal (*Julius Caesar*); or of romantic love in a world full of suffering (*Love's Labour's Lost*); or the difficulty of self-knowledge (*King Lear*); or of self-mastery (*The Tempest*).

Having examined individual plays along the lines suggested above the student of Shakespeare may feel the desire to trace the development of the great dramatist throughout the various stages of his career. As was mentioned at the beginning of this introductory chapter, each play apparently forms a landmark in the road along which Shakespeare the artist travelled and they all illuminate one another. From an examination of the different ways in which Shakespeare treated similar themes at different times in his life (for instance, from a comparison between *Romeo and Juliet* and *The Tempest*) we get an idea of the growth and development of his vision of life. However, as at the beginning we had to acknowledge our debt to scholars, so here too it is fitting to pay them a generous tribute. For by their indefatigable efforts they have managed to establish, though not altogether beyond any doubt, the chronology of Shakespeare's plays. Without knowledge of such chronology no study of the development of the poet's art and vision of life could be reliable, even if it were at all possible.

Finally, there is the study of Shakespearean criticism, that is the study of what critics wrote or said about Shakespeare, both in England and abroad. There are several reasons why the study of the critics of Shakespeare is both interesting and important. Such a study, to begin with, will help us towards a fuller understanding of him. In an essay on this subject T. S. Eliot wrote, 'When a poet is a great poet as Shakespeare is, we cannot judge of his greatness unaided; we need both the opinions of other poets and diverse views of critics who were not poets, in order to help us to understand'. Moreover, the study of Shakespearean criticism will help the curious among us to know how we have come to look upon Shakespeare in the way we do now. This is to say nothing of the importance of the history of Shakespearean criticism as a significant part of the history of literary taste, as a record of shifts in sensibility from Shakespeare's time to our own and as an essential part of the history of ideas. The same thing, to some extent, applies to the study of the stage productions of Shakespeare's plays across the ages. Likewise, the study of the fortunes of Shakespeare in countries other than England or English speaking countries, is interesting in itself as a record of the development of literary taste in these countries. It also helps to define the extent and significance of the universality of that great man.

2 Shakespeare the Man (1564—1616)

Very little is known for certain about the life of William Shakespeare. Apart from a handful of dates it is all largely a matter of conjecture or surmises. We are not even sure about the exact date of his birth. We know that he was baptised on 26 April 1564 at Stratford-upon-Avon in Warwickshire. This means that he must have been born not long before that date and there is more or less general agreement that he was born on or about 23 April. He was the third child of John and Mary Shakespeare whose first two children, both girls, died in infancy. His father, John Shakespeare, was a glover and wool merchant, prosperous enough to buy two houses in Stratford. His mother, Mary Arden, was the daughter of a well-to-do farmer who left her some land. For a number of years John Shakespeare played a prominent role in the municipal life of the town, he was chosen an alderman (one of the counsellors of the town) in 1565 and in 1568, when William was four years old, was elected bailiff (the equivalent of Mayor now) of Stratford, which was the highest civic honour in the town. Later, however, his fortunes changed and he was obliged, because of financial difficulties, to sell his wife's inheritance and mortgage part of his property. In 1573 he failed to pay a debt of £30 and a warrant for his arrest was issued. In 1577 he began to neglect his civic duties as alderman and in 1578 he was excused from paying his weekly contribution to the relief of the poor. Finally in 1587 he had to be replaced by a new alderman. Another relevant fact which may be mentioned here is that in 1592 his name appeared on a list of persons who did not go monthly to church 'according to her Majesties Lawes'. The alleged reason for his not going was fear of arrest for debt (in sixteenth century England such arrests could be made on Sundays).

William Shakespeare then was born into a well-to-do middle class type of family. Although his father ran into financial difficulties in the poet's early youth he was still in a position to keep his two houses as well as his business in Stratford. So there is no truth in the story, once popular, that the poet was born and brought up in poor circumstances. Nor was Stratford an obscure little village completely cut off from contemporary civilisation. The town had a good free school, the master of which was often a scholar and a graduate of Oxford, and, it has been pointed out he was not paid less than the masters at Eton. Some of the inhabitants of Stratford were men of learning who owned considerable libraries and during Shakespeare's early years visits by travelling theatrical companies were paid to the town almost every year. This point is stressed since the notion that Shakespeare was a poor and almost illiterate actor, who came from an insignificant little village, was largely responsible for the various attempts to attribute his plays to other authors.

It is not certain where Shakespeare received his education, but most scholars agree that he was probably sent by his father to the local free school where children went after learning to read and write. There they would study the Bible and mainly Latin works by Cato, Cicero, Caesar, especially Ovid and perhaps Virgil, Horace or Terence. The school syllabus would perhaps contain very little or no Greek. Boys would finish school at about fourteen or fifteen and after school they would go to university if they could afford it. According to tradition Shakespeare did not complete his studies, but had to leave school in order to help his father with his business. The amount of schooling Shakespeare would have had, according to this story, would accord with the estimate of his learning given by his great contemporary Ben Jonson, who referred to his 'little Latin and less Greek'. Ben Jonson, however, was a highly learned man and what *he* considered to be little might not be very little after all. In fact, impressed by Shakespeare's writings some scholars assume that he had a much better education than that afforded by the town free school. J. Dover Wilson, for instance, a great authority on the text of the plays, believes that the reason why Shakespeare's father did not go to church was not that he was afraid of being arrested for his debts, but that he was a Catholic, a member of the outlawed 'old religion'. Dover Wilson evolves the ingenious theory that as a Catholic Shakespeare's father could not have sent his son to the local grammar school to be taught by a Protestant schoolmaster and that Shakespeare 'received his early education as a singing-boy in the service of some great Catholic nobleman' (*The Essential Shakespeare*, p. 41, Cambridge University Press, 1932). This, according to Dover Wilson, might also explain why Shakespeare was at home in his description of the civilised life of the nobility. But surely the patronage of the Earl of Southampton at the beginning of the dramatist's career and the friendship which seems to have sprung up between the two men would be sufficient to account for Shakespeare's apparent knowledge of the life of the nobility.

The second date we have after Shakespeare's baptism is that of his marriage. Shakespeare was married in 1582, at the age of eighteen, to Anne Hathaway, who was eight years his senior. She bore him three children, Susanna born in 1583 and the twins Hamnet and Judith born in 1585. They were all baptised at the church in Stratford. After that date no records have been discovered relating to Shakespeare until we next hear of him in 1592 as a promising young dramatist doing well in London. We do not know whether he was recruited by a London company of players who happened to be visiting Stratford or he left for London alone in search of employment. There is a tradition, however, that he was obliged to leave Stratford because he was prosecuted for stealing a deer from the park of Sir Thomas Lucy and for composing a ballad in which he attacked him. Although poaching in those days was regarded as a wild sort of adventure which a young man might indulge in rather than as a serious offence, the story of deer-stealing remains unsubstantiated. Nor is it certain when he left, since the fact that his children were baptised in Stratford does not necessarily mean that he was there himself all the time.

What in fact happened in the intervening period between 1585 and 1592, when we are sure he was in London, is unknown, although several guesses have been made. Some believe a tradition which says that he worked as a schoolmaster in Stratford, helping to coach children and teach them the elements of reading and writing before they entered the grammar school. Others think that he must have been employed in a lawyer's office in London and this might account for his acquaintance with, and frequent use of, legal terms in his writings. Others, again, maintain that he must have been studying medicine or that he must have spent some time as a soldier fighting abroad. There is no end, in fact, to the guesses biographers indulge in and since Shakespeare's knowledge of human life is so wide and embraces so many walks of life, a biographer is almost certain to find in Shakespeare's works something that would seem to justify whatever fanciful theory he might devise.

The reference to Shakespeare's growing popularity on the London stage in 1592 occurs in a pamphlet written by a contemporary dramatist, Robert Greene (1560?–1592). Greene was one of a group of authors who had had a university education and were therefore known as The University Wits. He had been writing successful plays for the London theatrical companies for some time, but towards the end of his days he felt deserted by them and actually died in abject poverty. On his death bed he wrote the pamphlet or the address known as *Greenes Groats-worth of Wit* in which he warned his fellow University Wits, Marlowe, Peele and probably Nashe, who 'spend their wits in making plaies' not to trust actors, especially as among them there appeared then a writer, 'an upstart Crow, beautified with our feathers', who thought he was as good as the best of them, and who in fact constituted a real danger to them. For a number of reasons it is established beyond any doubt that the 'upstart Crow' was Shakespeare. In spite of the bitterness of Greene's attack, or perhaps because of it, it is reasonable to assume that Shakespeare was already a successful dramatist in 1592, which means that he must have started writing before that date. But the word 'upstart' suggests that his popularity was just beginning then. E. K. Chambers, his greatest biographer, puts the beginning of his dramaturgy as far back as 1591, and does not think that his career as an actor began long before 1592 (E. K. Chambers, *William Shakespeare. A Study of Facts and Problems*, Oxford at the Clarendon Press, 1930). There is a tradition, unsubstantiated until this day, that before he took up acting he used to take charge of horses at the playhouse door.

That Shakespeare was an actor is certain. His name is included in a list of actors for two of Ben Jonson's plays, *Every Man in His Humour* (1598) and *Sejanus* (1603). It also appears among the names of 'the principal actors' in 'all' the plays collected in the first edition of his works (the First Folio of 1623). However we have no reliable contemporary evidence concerning the quality of his acting or the parts he played. According to a later tradition he was at his best when playing the role of the ghost in his own play, *Hamlet*. There is another tradition which says that he played the part of Adam in *As You Like It*. It would seem, therefore, that he only played minor parts. There is no doubt, however, that he was keenly interested in the art and technique of acting, as we can easily tell from what he says on the subject through the lips of Hamlet, to say nothing of what is said in the other plays. We do not know which theatrical company Shakespeare first worked for, but from 1592 to 1594 he seemed to have written his first plays for three different companies. From 1594 to the rest of his career he wrote only for the leading company, known as The Lord Chamberlain's Men, later as The King's Men.

Shakespeare's career as actor and dramatist was at certain intervals interrupted by the closing of the theatres on account of plagues, which broke out only too easily in London. Such breaks enabled him to experiment with poetic forms other than drama. He published two long narrative poems, *Venus and Adonis* in 1593 and *The Rape of Lucrece* in 1594. Both were dedicated to the young nobleman, Henry Wriothesley, Earl of Southampton. The former poem he described in his dedicatory address as his first published work. The two poems established his reputation as a poet; they ran into several editions during his life time and until 1597, when some of the individual plays began to appear in print, were his only published works. About this time Shakespeare seemed to have had an unsuccessful love affair, but again this is not certain.

Most probably in 1595 (although some scholars put this date back two years) Shakespeare started writing the most personal of all his works, the sonnets, which he composed over a period of four or five years. Although the oldest edition extant bears the date 1609, the sonnets were already known and circulated in manuscript before that date. In 1598 Shakespeare was referred to as an author of 'sugared' sonnets by his contemporary and admirer, the priest and scholar Francis Meres. The sonnets are dedicated to 'Mr W. H.' who is described by the poet as 'the only begetter of these ensuing sonnets'. Scholars are not agreed on the identity of Mr W. H. Some assume that he was the young and handsome nobleman Henry Wriothesley, Earl of Southampton, who was nine years Shakespeare's junior and to whom his two narrative poems were also dedicated. Others maintain that he was

William Herbert, afterwards Earl of Pembroke, to whom the first collected edition of Shakespeare's plays, the First Folio, was subsequently dedicated by Shakespeare's fellow actors. Others, again, believe that he could not be either of these men, but another unknown person. In 1964 the Oxford historian A. L. Rowse suggested that Mr W. H. was the publisher's dedicatee, not Shakespeare's. Most of the sonnets are addressed to a young man, but some to a woman. If it is true that they are largely autobiographical we may gather from them that the poet had a deep affection and admiration for a young man and a passionate love for a dark woman who, however, betrayed him possibly with the same young man. Among the recent candidates suggested for the dark lady was Emilia Bassano, the daughter of an Italian musician, who was once the Lord Chamberlain's mistress.

The sonnets, the two narrative poems and one short poem, *The Phoenix and the Turtle*, written in honour of a certain Sir John Salisbury (printed in 1601) seem to be the only poetry Shakespeare had the time to write other than what is found in the plays. As for the poems ascribed to him, *The Passionate Pilgrim* and *A Lover's Complaint*, their authenticity is doubted by scholars. Playwriting and acting seem to have occupied all his time and when we consider that during his active career he wrote thirty-seven plays at the average rate of two plays a year, we are not a bit surprised that he had precious little time to write anything else. Nor are we surprised to find him, after those full and exhausting years, retiring to his native town at a relatively young age, when he seemed to be still at the height of his creative power.

Shakespeare rose to prosperity rapidly. In 1595 he became a sharer in the company of The Lord Chamberlain's Men. He and others were paid on behalf of their company for dramatic performances given at court in the winter of the preceding year. Under Queen Elizabeth his company was most favoured at court, and when King James succeeded to the throne it was singled out for the honour of the name The King's Men. Its members were made officers of the royal household and were allowed to perform in any part of the country. On one particular occasion Shakespeare and his fellows wore their red liveries in a royal procession. According to Ben Jonson both Elizabeth and James liked Shakespeare's plays. There is the tradition that Shakespeare wrote *The Merry Wives of Windsor* (in a fortnight) because the

Queen had expressed the desire to see Falstaff in love, after having seen, and greatly admired, Shakespeare's portrayal of this character in *Henry IV*. Besides, although *Richard II*, which deals with the deposition of a king, was played by Shakespeare's company at the command of some of the followers of the Earl of Essex just before his unfortunate and abortive rising, the company was given orders to perform again at court only a fortnight after the incident.

During his active career Shakespeare lived in London, first in Bishopsgate and later in Southwark, near the theatres for which he worked. The most famous of these theatres was 'The Globe', built in 1599, of which Shakespeare was a part-owner. However, Shakespeare did not sever his link with Stratford. In 1597 he had saved enough money to buy the second largest mansion in Stratford, The New Place. A year earlier his father, most probably with his son's financial aid, had applied for a family coat of arms, which was granted to him. In 1602 Shakespeare bought a large piece of land near Stratford for the sum of £320, which was a substantial amount of money in those days (the equivalent of a great many thousands now) and in 1605 he invested there a further sum of £440. It was not, however, as an author, but as an actor and especially as a company shareholder that Shakespeare managed to make this fortune. (The average fee an author was paid for the script of a play was not much more than six pounds, and it was not unusual for authors to die as penniless as Robert Greene.) Shakespeare, in fact, was not the only member of his company to make money. Others, like Augustine Phillips and Henry Condell, saved enough to buy property too.

Shakespeare spent the last years of his life in retirement in Stratford, where he seemed to have moved in 1610. But he did not lose all ties with his company in London. While in Stratford he still wrote plays for The King's Men, but they were not many, and after 1613 he stopped writing altogether. He made a few visits to London, but apparently to conclude business transactions or in connection with a lawsuit in which he was involved as a witness. On one occasion (in 1613) he had to go there in order to design a shield to be painted by Burbage for the Earl of Rutland to carry at a royal tournament.

It seems that Shakespeare led a very quiet life at Stratford. No records have as yet been unearthed to show that he took any important part in the municipal life of the town. He died on 23 April 1616, having made his final will on 25 March. There is a popular story recorded about the middle of the seventeenth century, which says that Shakespeare died of a fever he contracted while drinking heavily at a reunion with his old fellow poets, Drayton and Ben Jonson. In his will, which is one of the few documents on which Shakespeare's signature is preserved, there are small bequests to the poor and to his sometime fellow actors, Burbage, Heminges and Condell, to buy themselves rings to wear in his memory. His property was left to the various members of his family. Shakespeare's hope of founding a family, made clear in his will, was not realised. His son Hamnet died in 1596. His elder daughter Susanna married the local physician, John Hall, in 1607 and had a daughter, Elizabeth, who had no children. Judith married the son of the Bailiff of Stratford, Thomas Quiney, in 1616 but all their children died, the last in 1639.

Shakespeare's body was buried in the church at Stratford-upon-Avon, which has now become the Mecca of all Shakespeare admirers. His remains have not been exhumed because on the tomb stone there is a simple verse inscription that lays a curse upon anybody who would move his bones. On the poet's monument there is a bust carved by Gheerart Janssen, an artist of Flemish origin, above which there is reproduced the family coat of arms.

What manner of man was Shakespeare? His great contemporary, Ben Jonson, refers to him more than once as 'gentle' and the word is also used by his fellow actors, Heminges and Condell, when they speak of him. He seems to have worked with his colleagues for twenty years without a serious quarrel. In an age when people were generally irascible and lost their temper only too easily (Marlowe was stabbed to death in a fight and Ben Jonson had to go to jail and was nearly brought to the gallows) he must have possessed a sober temperament and a balanced character. He generally avoided getting involved in dangerous political issues and taking sides in the endless quarrels that raged between the contending theatrical companies and the play-wrights of the time. In London his life may not have been altogether above reproach but he obviously took his family responsibilities seriously. Despite what must have been great temptations in those boisterous days he could not have led a wild and riotous life like some of his contemporaries, otherwise he would not have been able to make a fortune. On the contrary, the greatest English poet, it seems, was also a sober and shrewd business man. His will shows that he was a man faithful to his friends, just as his friends' praise of him, attached to the First Folio, reveals the extent and depth of their affection for him. Although his plays were well received at the Court he did not stoop to flatter the reigning monarch. Nor did he waste his creative gift in writing occasional verses. Shakespeare must have been a modest man to an astonishing degree—how else can we account for the fact that he, the world's greatest playwright, did not publish his complete works, like, for instance, his contemporary Ben Jonson? Nevertheless, his plays, no less than his sonnets, show that he had great respect for his art and that he fully realised the dignity of the poet's calling.

3 The Social Background of the Plays

The beginning of the Tudor dynasty, of whom the last and greatest member was Queen Elizabeth, marked the end of the civil wars in England (1455–1485) about which Shakespeare wrote four of his history plays. The civil wars, known as the Wars of the Roses, fought between the two royal houses, York and Lancaster, were brought to an end with the defeat of the Yorkist King Richard III in the battle of Bosworth Field in 1485. Richard lost his life while heroically fighting for his crown, and Henry Tudor, Earl of Richmond, who claimed descent from the house of Lancaster, then became king. By marrying Elizabeth of York, Henry, now called Henry VII, managed to end the old feud between the two contending houses.

Important changes occurred in the structure of English society during the Tudor period. Indeed some of these changes had started a long time before, but their far reaching implications revealed themselves fully under the Tudor monarchs. It hardly needs to be said that to understand Shakespeare's plays it is necessary to know something about the structure of the society in which Shakespeare lived. But to get a clear picture of this it is useful to know something about the way English society was composed in the previous period, that is, the Middle Ages. The Tudor period witnessed the transition of English society from the Middle Ages to the Renaissance and the full flowering of the Renaissance itself. Although we now know that there was much more in common between Shakespeare's or Renaissance England and medieval England than people used to think, there were still many significant differences between them. Besides, some of Shakespeare's plays (*King John*, *Richard II*, *Henry IV*, *Henry V*, *Henry VI* and *Richard III*) are set in medieval England. Shakespeare, it is true, does not faithfully observe in them the details of medieval life, he does not always distinguish between life in his own time and that of the past, and his interpretation of the events in them is, quite rightly, not medieval, but Elizabethan and even Shakespearean. After all Shakespeare was not a historian, but a dramatic artist. Yet the structure of society which these plays portray is, in its basic features, medieval. Unless it is explained to him, the student is apt to be bewildered, for instance, by the presence of the Pope's Legate and the cardinals; he may not understand why bishops and archbishops keep appearing on the political scene and meddling in political issues, or how it is possible for the crown to be bandied about like a tennis ball from one party to another. These are matters that do not perplex a Western or an English student acquainted with the social and political history of his country, but they tend to be a source of confusion for others.

England in the Middle Ages was not so much an independent state or nation in the modern sense as a part of Western Europe, which in those days was known as Christendom. Since it was an agricultural community its social structure was defined by its system of land tenure, which, like the rest of Europe, was feudal. Reduced to its basic formula English feudalism, which was introduced by William the Conqueror and developed by Henry II, meant that all the land belonged to the king who disposed of it as he pleased. The king divided most of it among his barons, his tenants-in-chief, who, in return, were to pay him certain fees and supply him with knights and men to fight for him in time of war. In their turn, these nobles gave land or *feudum* to their vassals, the knights who swore allegiance to them in life and death. The king ruled the country indirectly through his lords and barons and directly by means of his sheriff, an officer of baronial rank whom he appointed in every shire. The baron's function, therefore, was to be both the king's lieutenant in war and his counsellor in peace. Each of the estates or holdings belonging to a lord was called a manor and in it was built originally a castle, later a mansion or manor-house. The lord was a magnate in his district and kept a large retinue of knights to defend him. This explains why in certain periods of English history the nobility became so powerful that, instead of fighting for their king, they challenged his authority and even waged war on him.

Keeping the balance between the power of the king and that of the barons there was the medieval church, which, directed by the Pope in Rome, dominated the whole of Europe. The Church was immensely rich and in England it held much land from the king. In their functions and their way of life clergymen then were quite different from what they are now. Many of them did not carry out the pastoral duties of priests and performed jobs that had nothing to do with religion as we now know it. They worked as civil servants, statesmen, doctors, lawyers and private secretaries. They were not allowed to marry, but, on the other hand, they enjoyed many privileges, the most important of which was that offenders among them were tried by a special ecclesiastical court and not by the king's court.

Clergymen were roughly divided into two classes, the lower and the higher strata. The former included the ordinary parish priest, who was often of peasant origin, who farmed a piece of land belonging to the Church. He was the sole source of religious information for his parishioners. Because the Church was the centre of the activities of the community the priest or parson played an important role in the village social life, for instance, he organised the parish play, the performance of which was an exciting event in the life of the village. Together with the parish priest there was often the chantry priest, whose job was to perform services for the souls of the dead and he often kept a free school where he taught reading and writing and some Latin. To the same class of clergy belonged the friar who was a mendicant itinerant clergyman travelling from one village to another, preaching and begging his keep, and the ordinary monks and nuns who led a life of contemplation behind the walls of monasteries and convents.

The parish priests were governed by the bishops and their deputies, the archdeacons. The archdeacons visited parishes periodically, held religious courts, inquired into religious offences and sent 'summoners' with letters of summons to offenders. Above all the clergy the Pope reigned supreme. Although far away he was a dominant presence in the minds of the people, who regarded him as their 'Father on earth'. Occasionally the 'pardoner' visited the parish to collect money payments for the Pope, which, the people were told, would be counted among their good deeds and would, therefore, lessen their punishment in purgatory. The Pope also received much money from England in other ways, for instance, all newly appointed clergymen had to pay him their first income from their posts. He also had his ambassador in

England, a powerful and influential man of the rank of cardinal, called the Pope's Legate. In the Middle Ages this office was held by the Archbishop of Canterbury.

The bishops and archbishops belonged to the higher strata of clergymen. They were exceedingly wealthy. For instance, in the early Tudor period the income of the two archbishops (of Canterbury and of York) was about £3000 each, while the richest landowner in the country did not receive more than £6000. The clergy had their own parliament, the Convocation, and the higher clergy were elected on the nomination of the Pope. However, the king also had a say in the matter, for he rewarded his clerics in the government service by giving them higher and more lucrative positions in the Church. The English bishops had their mansions in London and they either attended the king or acted as his ambassadors abroad. The higher clergymen then performed the functions of higher civil servants in the state and that was natural in an age when they were the only learned people. It is not surprising then that clergymen meddled with politics. In *Henry IV* we see the Archbishop of York rising against the king and supporting the rebels. Unlike the nobility, the ecclesiastical hierarchy did not depend on birth and heredity. By sheer industry a talented man of humble origin might work his way up to the highest position in the Church. A well known example is furnished by the career of Wolsey, who became, in Shakespeare's words, 'the prime man of the State' in the reign of Henry VIII.

What was the position of the common man in the Middle Ages? The peasant who cultivated the estates of the nobility and the Church was a mere serf or slave or as he was called a villein or a bondman. He and his family belonged by birth to the estate and were not free to leave it. His exact status was half way between a slave and a free labourer. He had to support himself and his family by working in his free time on a strip of land which he held from his lord by what was known as villein tenure. His main task, however, was to till the lord's land, which he did under the supervision of the lord's bailiff and his assistant, the reeve. The bailiff acted as a middleman between the lord and his villein tenants. He attended to the letting of land and other important matters like the holding of manor-courts which settled disputes between lord and villeins. The reeve, who was chosen from the tenants by the tenants, helped in supervising the work of the peasants in the lord's fields. The villeins who did not hold any land worked as day-labourers and were given a certain pay, but they were still as unfree as the rest. As for the few 'free-holders', that is, those farmers holding their land directly from the king, they were regarded as free men although many of them had to do some services for their lord. Their land descended to their heirs and they were free to leave the manor, give their daughters in marriage without the lord's permission and even sublet their land. In the beginning of feudal society the villeins constituted by far the majority of the population but for political, social, and economic reasons by the beginning of the Tudor reign they were very much the exception. They became either the 'yeomen farmers' or else the landless labourers.

That was the position of the common man in the medieval village, which was a manor belonging to some lord, secular or ecclesiastical. The medieval village was a self-contained, self-sufficient unit. It had its own industry, its craftsmen (and their apprentices) who were either villeins or small freeholders. But in the course of time some villages grew larger and more important than others, and these eventually became towns or as they were then called 'boroughs'. The boroughs gradually won certain rights from their lords denied to villages, the most important of which was the right of self-government. This consisted in the administering of justice and the passing of by-laws by the burgesses in the 'Courthouse' or 'Guildhall'. To be a burgess a man had to be a master in his craft or else he had to be sufficiently wealthy to purchase the right. From the burgesses aldermen and chamberlains were elected. Craftsmen formed themselves into guilds by the mayor's permission and a man could only enter a guild on completion of his apprenticeship, that is, when he became a freeman or master or a fully qualified workman and if he could afford the entrance fees for the guild. Each guild performed for its members many social and welfare services which often included the acting of a play. This was sometimes an important social event in the life of a borough and some guilds, like those of Coventry and Chester, had their chief annual festival on the day they performed their play.

Such, in brief, was the social picture of England in the Middle Ages. The king, the barons or peers of the realm and the bishops or peers of the Church ruled over the land and the whole system was one of a rigid hierarchy and of legal subordination of villeins to lords. Among the villagers and townspeople corporate life was all-important, as can be seen in their submission to the Church and to the medieval guild. On the whole it was not a system that encouraged much individuality. But towards the end of the Middle Ages there were many forces at work that resulted in the disintegration of the medieval structure of society. The feudal manor had gone and, although the system of villein tenure was sometimes kept in a modified form, the villein status itself was disappearing very rapidly. New social classes began to emerge thus bridging the gap between the lords and the villeins. Trade, especially export cloth trade, was developing beyond the capacity and resources of the traditional guilds. Boroughs or towns, especially London, were growing rapidly in size and importance. The introduction of printing helped to spread learning among the laymen who were, as a result, beginning to think and form their independent judgment on religious as well as other matters. Whereas in the Middle Ages the village or borough was a self-contained unit, to which the inhabitant's loyalties were confined, the Tudors managed to weld together villages and boroughs into one whole nation thus heightening the feeling of nationalism to an unprecedented degree. The disappearance of medieval dialects and the gradual emergence and dominance of the London dialect as the standard Enlgish also helped to break down the barriers between one region of the country and another.

However, the Tudor period still inherited from the Middle Ages its conception of social hierarchy, although there were now more classes and a much freer intercourse between them. An examination of Tudor society shows that it was composed of the following ranks or classes, all of which appear in Shakespeare's plays.

THE KING AND THE PEERS OF THE REALM

The Wars of the Roses had a profound effect on the position of the nobility — they lost all their independent military and a good deal of their political power. Many lords were killed in battle or forfeited their large estates. Henry VII and his son

Henry VIII did not lavishly create new lords and during their reigns the once overmighty lords were replaced by men who had proved their loyalty to the king. The monarch became more autocratic in his rule, he chose any of his subjects whom he could trust to be a member of his council and convened Parliament (which consisted of the nobility, the higher clergy, judges and eminent townsmen) only to ratify his decisions. Instead of the sheriffs he made much use of the justices of the peace (JPs) (like Master Shallow in *Henry VI Part 1*), who under the supervision of the king's 'Privy Council', saw to it that the king's policy was carried out throughout the realm. They were a committee of local gentry chosen annually by the king to carry out the task of local government in each county. They were only part time administrators and were paid a nominal salary. But any gentleman with social and political ambitions aspired to be appointed to the Commission of the Peace. During the Elizabethan period the JPs became most influential because of the political, economic and administrative powers they enjoyed. The Tudors had no standing army, but each locality had to supply a number of men, already trained and fully armed, for the Militia. Under Elizabeth the sheriff as commander and organiser of the militia in each shire was replaced by a county officer called the Lord Lieutenant. In *Henry IV* we find Falstaff empowered by the justice of the peace to press men for the wars. The Tudor monarch governed the country through his council of twenty or thirty men, his six or seven hundred justices of the peace and only occasionally through Parliament.

Since many of Shakespeare's plays are set in courts a word about life at the Elizabethan court is included. The court in London was both the Queen's residence and the seat of government. There the Queen was attended most of the year by the nobility, who beside their various manor houses had their mansions in London. The royal household was a most elaborate organisation, but as Shakespeare's plays do not on the whole show the author's familiarity with it we need not bother to explain it here. Suffice it to say, however, that the Tudor monarch was personally attended by the Gentlemen (or Ladies or Gentlewomen) of the Privy Chamber. Every night two of the Gentlemen (or Gentlewomen) were required to sleep in the Privy Chamber. We may note that in *Macbeth* King Duncan has two such gentlemen sleeping with him in Macbeth's castle. Unlike what is sometimes seen in the plays, the monarch was rarely unattended. For instance, when Shakespeare shows us Claudius alone at prayer he is obviously deviating from Tudor custom, or deliberately simplifying the royal set up of his time for the sake of the exigencies of the plot — although, as has been pointed out by a scholar, when he makes Hamlet pass through the King's Chamber to get to the Queen's Shakespeare proves that he knows well the architecture of a Tudor palace.

The atmosphere of the Elizabethan court was one of brilliance and gaiety, though not devoid of tragedy and political intrigue. At the court a young man learnt how to develop a taste for scholarship and the fine arts, especially poetry, music and dancing. The medieval view of the almost illiterate nobleman who, compared with the learned clerk, cared mainly for martial valour was now replaced by the Renaissance ideal of the all round gentleman, of whom Sir Philip Sidney provided a living example in real life and Prince Hamlet is an embodiment in art — the person who is at once a courtier, a soldier and a scholar. One of the striking features of the Court of Elizabeth (and of her successor James I), which is revealed in contemporary descriptions, is its fondness for colour, pomp and ceremony. Here is an excerpt from a contemporary description of the Queen at her palace at Greenwich written by a foreigner (Paul Hentzner, *Travels in England*, 1598):

At the door (of the Presence-Chamber) stood a gentleman dressed in velvet, with a gold chain, whose office was to introduce to the Queen any person of distinction that came to wait on her. It was Sunday, when there is usually the greatest attendance of nobility. In the same hall were the Archbishop of Canterbury, the Bishop of London, a great number of counsellors of state, officers of the Crown, and gentlemen who waited the Queen's coming out, which she did from her own apartment when it was time to go to prayers, attended in the following manner:-

First went gentlemen, barons, earls, knights of the Garter, all richly dressed and bareheaded; next came the Lord High Chancellor of England, bearing the seals in a red silk purse, between two, one of whom carried the royal sceptre, the other

the sword of state, in a red scabbard, studded with golden
fleur-de-lis, the point upwards; next came the Queen . . . upon
her head she had a small crown, reported to be made of some of
the gold of the celebrated Luneburg table . . . and she had a
necklace of exceeding fine jewels . . . That day she was dressed
in white silk, bordered with pearls of the size of beans, and over
it a mantle of black silk shot with silver threads; her train was
very long, the end of it borne by a marchioness; instead of a
chain, she had an oblong collar of gold and jewels . . . Wherever
she turned her face as she was going along, everybody fell down
on their knees. The ladies of the court followed next to her,
very handsome and well-shaped, and for the most part dressed
in white. She was guarded on each side by the gentlemen
pensioners, fifty in number, with gilt halberds . . . In the chapel
was excellent music; as soon as it and the service were over,
which scarcely exceeded half-an-hour, the Queen returned in
the same state and order, and prepared to go to dinner. (See J.
D. Wilson, *Life in Shakespeare's England*, pp. 244–46, Pelican
Books, 1949.)

Shakespeare, it is true, may not have been acquainted with the
intricate and complicated details of life at the court, but he must
have seen something of this pomp and ceremony, at least when he
acted before the Queen at Greenwich in 1594. Besides, court
masques, especially during the reign of James I, were very
frequent and any Londoner could see the breath-takingly colourful processions of masquers in the streets of the capital on their
way to the royal palace. The pomp and ceremony of which
Shakespeare wrote were not, therefore, a mere abstract notion, but
a concrete reality, which the poet could not help but see in actual
life. At the court (and outside it) people, including men, were
richly and lavishly dressed. Foreign visitors commented on it and
puritans attacked it.

It was at the court that fashions were born and were soon
discarded when they were imitated by 'the common people' in the
city and the country and even by actors. Contemporary authors
remarked, often with disapproval, on the speed at which clothes
went out of fashion; the multiplicity of fashions derived not only
from Italy and France, but even from Turkey and Morocco. In
1593 Thomas Nashe described England as 'the players' stage of

gorgeous attire, the ape of all nations' superfluities, the continual masquers in outlandish habilements'. Because men, no less than women, wore chains, rings (and ear rings), jewels, pearls and precious stones, they often spent vast sums of money on these jewels and their costly appearance became the theme of satir cal attacks not only by Shakespeare, but by most of his contemporaries. Often the Elizabethan dandy was a much travelled man who was anxious to make his fellow countrymen realise that he had been abroad, looked down upon what was native and punctuated his conversation with foreign expressions. In short, he was the type that Shakespeare made Rosalinde call 'Monsieur Traveller' in *As You Like It*, and that he attacked in many of his plays, notably through the lips of Mercutio in *Romeo and Juliet* and of Hamlet. Wearing swords was considered part of the full dress of a nobleman in civil life – a privilege which was extended to 'gentlemen'. Duelling and fencing (such as we find in *Romeo and Juliet* and *Hamlet*) were beginning to be fashionable, and since fencing was a foreign art most of the terms used in it were foreign.

Shakespeare has left us many portraits of young noble gallants who often go about in groups of three, as we find in *Love's Labour's Lost* (Berowne, Longaville and Dumain), in *Romeo and Juliet* (Romeo, Mercutio and Benvolio) and in *Much Ado About Nothing* (Don Pedro, Benedick and Claudio). It has been suggested that the original of these portraits was perhaps the poet's patron, the young nobleman Earl of Southampton, whom he seems to have known fairly intimately. It is, in fact, the life of the nobility rather than life at the royal court with which Shakespeare seems to have been familiar. The picture he has drawn of life at the household of the Elizabethan nobility, as is clearly seen in Olivia's household in *Twelfth Night*, is we are told not very far from the truth. In splendour the palaces and mansions owned by dukes, marquesses earls and barons were generally smaller versions of the royal court. Although on the whole the Tudor monarchs curbed the political power of the nobility they did not wish to lessen the importance of their role in social life. The nobility kept a large retinue wearing their livery. In 1598 John Stowe, in his book *A Survey of London*, wrote that the Earl of Derby had a retinue of 220 and that the Earl of Oxford used to ride to his house in London with eighty gentlemen in a livery of Reading tawny, and chains of gold about their necks before him, and one hundred tall yeomen in the like livery to follow him without chains, but all having his cognisance of the blue boar embroidered on their left shoulder.

This may help us realise how painful it is for Lear to have his retinue cut by half, or reduced in the way his daughters suggest.

The household of a nobleman was not so intricate in its organisation as the royal household. Nevertheless, it had an enormous staff among whom was observed a hierachy of positions similar to that at the court. There were the gentlemen-in-waiting (and the gentlewomen) as well as the yeomen servants. At the head of the household was the steward, who was responsible for all financial matters, for the provisioning, the necessary repairs and the discipline of the staff. In one particular case the steward was responsible for a staff of 80 gentlemen and 500 yeomen. The steward, therefore, was a gentleman, sometimes a knight or a scholar and the gentlemen (and gentlewomen)-in-waiting were often gentle by birth. Maria, in *Twelfth Night*, is, therefore, not a chamber maid but a gentlewoman (who knows how to write and even imitate her mistress's handwriting) and there is nothing shocking or improbable in her marrying a knight, who is her lady's relation, Sir Toby Belch. Nor was anything shocking in a noble lady's marrying one of her gentlemen-in-waiting, although Malvolio was not a little exaggerating when he said that he knew of a certain lady who married her *yeoman* of the wardrobe. After the gentlemen of the household came the yeomen servants and the grooms responsible for various things like the pantry, cellar, bakehouse, kitchen, wardrobe and stables. To a noble household also belonged secretaries, schoolmasters and chaplains. The noblemen had a large number of dependents. In their halls scores of people ate every day, and these often included scholars. In this way Tudor hospitality, or 'housekeeping' as it was called, helped to maintain general culture. On the whole, the nobility encouraged learning and the arts and gave their protection and patronage to companies of actors who bore their names.

THE CLERGY AND THE PEERS OF THE CHURCH

The position of the clergy suffered an ever greater change in the

Tudor period. It was during the reign of Henry VIII that the movement known as the Reformation of the Church took place. Henry wanted the Pope to declare null his marriage to his first wife, Katherine of Aragon, but the Pope did not think it was right to grant him his request, especially as Katherine's nephew was the mighty King of Spain, whom he could not afford to offend. As a result Henry managed to pass through Parliament a series of acts (between 1529 and 1535) which severed all ties between the Church of England and Rome, and made him the supreme head of the English Church. Bishops now were elected from those nominated by the king instead of the Pope. In 1536 he dissolved monasteries and their rich estates passed to the Crown though ultimately they were sold to the gentry. Of course, it would be entirely wrong to attribute the Reformation of the Church solely to the king's desire to obtain Papal permission to rid himself of his wife; in reality this was only the occasion which precipitated the breach with Rome and without the presence of other and more significant factors the king would have met with much greater opposition. The movement was partly a manifestation of the spirit of nationalism that began to make itself felt in England at the time and which developed half a century later into the wave of patriotism that swept the whole country. Together with resentment of foreign interference there was widespread discontent with the abuses of the Church, which derived part of its power from Rome and from its partial independence of the king. The luxury in which the higher clergy lived was the object of many an attack and in *Henry VIII* Shakespeare has given us an example of the lavish and splendid parties Cardinal Wolsey gave in his palace. The clergy also aroused the envy and hostility of the other classes, especially the gentry who were becoming much wealthier, more powerful and better educated than before. Now with the spread of learning there were many well-educated lawyers and gentlemen who felt they were capable of doing the secretarial work hitherto done exclusively by the clergy and bishops and who could, therefore, hold the important government offices confined to the clergy. Then there was the impact of the teachings of Luther and his Protestant followers (that is, the people who 'protested' against the abuses of the Church and wanted to return to a purer and simpler religion). In this connection the effect of the printed translations of the Bible was profound indeed in stimulating individual judgment.

By the close of Henry VIII's reign the Church in England had been fundamentaly altered. It came directly under the king's control. Instead of the medieval Latin service, an English liturgy was used, and there was now a copy of the English Bible in every church in the country. It is true that Catholicism, the old religion, was restored by Henry's daughter, Queen Mary and with it the power of the Pope. She persecuted many Protestants and reintroduced the Pope's Legate. But Mary only reigned for five years, and when Queen Elizabeth succeeded her to the throne she freed the Church of England once and for all from foreign domination, permitted the clergy to marry, altered the prayer book in some respects to satisfy the Catholics and made it compulsory for people to go to church (Shakespeare's father, for instance, was fined for failing to go to church). In 1563 the Pope forbade the Catholics to attend the English Church and in 1570 he excommunicated Queen Elizabeth and declared her subjects free to disobey her. The result was a series of Catholic plots to overthrow her, in which were implicated a number of ardent Catholic Englishmen trained by the Jesuits abroad. There was also for many years the threat of an invasion by Spain, which, having concluded peace with France and now in league with the Pope, wanted to subject England to Spanish supremacy and reintroduce in it Roman Catholicism. In 1588 the mighty Spanish fleet, the Armada, did actually attempt to invade Britain, but was defeated. It is against this background of political unrest, of fear of possible invasion and outbreak of civil war that Shakespeare's history plays should be considered. For instance, the patriotism of *Henry V* or the hostile attitude to the Pope in *King John* can be explained in the light of these facts.

Another significant change in the position of the clergy, which can most clearly be seen in the Elizabethan age, was that they no longer occupied the most influential posts in the state. For instance, Elizabeth's Privy Council, that is, the body of men holding the leading government offices, consisted almost exclusively of laymen. In Parliament there were many more temporal than spiritual peers in the House of Lords. This secularisation of the government, together with making the monarch the head of both Church and state and the rising spirit of nationalism may account for the birth of the phenomenon of the near worship of the ruler or the king — which is one of the themes Shakespeare treated in some of his plays.

Under Queen Elizabeth the clergy were no longer envied or hated. In state matters they were kept subordinate to the laity. The archbishops felt subordinate to the Queen's secretary, William Cecil, and even in the country the parish priest felt inferior to the esquire. In fact, priests were sometimes almost looked down upon; for instance, we notice in Shakespeare's *Love's Labour's Lost* a condescending attitude to the priest. At the end of Elizabeth's reign Anglicanism (or the Church of England) had become the religion of the majority, although there were many puritans (people who were extreme Protestants and followers of Calvin's teachings) who did not accept the state's control of religion, objected to having bishops in the Church and thought that religion was a matter of private conscience. Among the puritans were many clergymen, justices of the peace, leading London merchants and even members of the Privy Council. They tried to force the Queen to move further in the direction of Protestantism, but, afraid of causing a civil war between the Protestants and the Catholics, the Queen preferred to steer a middle course and keep the Church of England, as it was, a compromise. In Shakespeare's time, then, religion was not separate from politics. The Queen saw that in both the sermon he gave, and the homily (printed by the Church) he read to his congregation, the priest helped to create the orthodox religious and, therefore, political beliefs among them.

THE KNIGHTS, ESQUIRES AND GENTLEMEN

Like the titles of the nobility the order of knighthood was conferred only by the king, but unlike them it was not hereditary. It was confined to a small number of the rural upper class. The order was not so much an indication of a whole social class as a title of honour conferred by the monarch as a reward for some great service, military or otherwise. The knight had the title 'Sir' prefixed to his name as in Sir John Falstaff or Sir Toby Belch.

As for the rank of esquire, originally it came immediately below that of knight, but later and especially during the Elizabethan reign anybody from the untitled landed class could become an esquire on application (and payment) for a coat of arms to the Herald's Office. Having a coat of arms was, therefore, the official sign of gentility. (We know that in 1596 Shakespeare's father, for instance, applied for a coat of arms, which he was granted in 1599.) An esquire would have added to his name the word esquire or gentleman. During the Elizabethan age, according to the English social historian G. M. Trevelyan, the esquire became 'the principal figure in the life of the countryside' (G. M. Trevelyan, *English Social History*, Longmans, Green & Co., London, 1942). The country 'gentlemen' had acquired much wealth by buying from the Crown much land that had once belonged to the monasteries and now that the feudal lords and the abbots of monasteries had gone the importance of the esquires increased considerably. From this class of gentlemen justices of the peace were usually chosen. The ranks of the landed gentry were continually replenished by prosperous merchants and especially by lawyers who often amassed much wealth in those days. Most of these merchants and lawyers, however, were brought up as younger sons of 'gentlemen' and were forced to leave their father's estates to make their fortunes in trade or the law by the custom of primogeniture, which made the first born son the sole heir to an estate.

Like the nobility the gentlemen had their own manor-houses, which of course were, as a rule, much smaller than the rural palaces belonging to the nobility. Like them also, they had their own deer parks for purposes of hunting, which was described by a contemporary author as the 'most royal' recreation. They bred many varieties of dogs and many treatises written on hunting point out the subtleties of the art of matching the cries of hounds. (There is nothing particularly erudite, therefore, about Shakespeare's ennumeration of the various kinds and degrees of dogs in *Macbeth* III i 93ff.) Because of the spread of such deer parks, poaching deer was a common sport among the young, especially the university students. Whereas the gentlemen hunted the deer, those beneath them hunted the hare. Hawking also was popular among the gentry (and this explains Shakespeare's frequent use of imagery derived from hawking). Unlike the nobility the gentlemen, as a rule, did not adorn their houses with paintings, except perhaps family portraits. But the walls of their rooms were covered with rich tapestry, arras and painted cloth depicting scenes and figures from the Bible and classical mythology. On the whole the knights and esquires were a prosperous class and kept up the tradition of hospitality or housekeeping. For instance, the poet John Donne belonged for some time to the household of a knight.

Although a coat of arms was the official sign of gentility, according to an Elizabethan author, the title 'gentleman' was not in common usage confined to the rich landed classes. In *De Republica Anglorum* (published in 1583) Sir Thomas Smith wrote:

> Whosoever studieth the laws of the realm, professeth liberal sciences, and to be short, who can live idly and without manual labour, and will bear the port, charge and countenance of a gentleman, he shall be called master, for that is the title which men give to esquires and other gentlemen, and shall be taken for gentleman.

THE YEOMEN

These were the class of farmers holding a middle position between the knights and esquires above and the farm labourers and husbandmen below. According to Sir Thomas Smith, a yeoman is 'a freeman born English' who has an income from his freeland of about six Elizabethan pounds. Unlike the gentlemen they did their own farming themselves or with the help of servants and indeed they even farmed the land belonging to gentlemen. Sometimes they became wealthy enough to buy more land and send their children to the universities or to study law and leave them enough land to enable them to live without labour, thus their sons might themselves become gentlemen. Among his neighbours a yeoman would have prefixed to his name the title 'goodman' as in 'Goodman Brown', but more officially the word yeoman is added to the name as in the case of 'John Brown, Yeoman'.

The yeomen were praised by Elizabethan authors for their valour and skill in archery. A notable example is to be found in Shakespeare's *Henry V*.

CITIZENS AND BURGESSES

With the vast increase of the English export cloth trade and the rise of the importance of towns, the Tudor town or borough became relatively more distinct from the village, although the difference between them was not so great as it is now. By the end of Queen Elizabeth's reign more than four-fifths of the population of England and Wales (which reached about four millions) lived in the country. Towns were small and, beside their business, burgesses had their free holdings and were partly engaged in agriculture. Farmsteads and shops were found side by side. It was, therefore, natural that, although born in a town, Shakespeare was familiar with life in the country (and even with wildlife in the forest, since Stratford-upon-Avon was not far from the romantic forest of Arden, which became the setting of one of his delightful comedies, *As You Like It*). Burgesses who held civic positions were men of some substance, and to this class of burgesses belonged Shakespeare's father, who became an alderman and for some time bailiff of Stratford-upon-Avon. We find this class of burgesses (together with gentlemen, yeomen and labourers) in the plays that deal basically with Elizabethan middle class life, like *The Merry Wives of Windsor*, *The Comedy of Errors* and *The Taming of the Shrew*. In the order of social significance citizens and burgesses occupy a middle position between gentlemen and yeomen.

One of the more important social changes that occurred in the boroughs under the Tudors (or more precisely towards the end of the Middle Ages) was that the inhabitants became sharply divided into two classes: the wealthy merchants and businessmen (and the lawyers and the professional class) and the poorer class of small craftsmen and artisans. Under the medieval system of guilds both the master craftsman and his apprentices and journeymen worked and even lived and ate together in an atmosphere of social equality. But now this social equality disappeared as a result of the emergence of the powerful capitalist entrepreneur (symbol of the growing individualism of the times) who managed the vastly expanding export cloth trade. The rich merchants, especially those of London, became exceedingly influential and together with the landed gentry, some of whom were originally businessmen, ruled the country.

THE WAGE-EARNING CLASS

The poorer inhabitants of towns, like farm labourers in villages, were the lowest social class in Elizabethan society, the class which Sir Thomas Smith describes as the 'fourth sort of men which do not rule' (after the Gentlemen, Citizens and Burgesses and Yeomen). These, according to him, include, 'day-labourers, poor husbandmen [farmers], yea merchants and retailers which have no free land, copyholders [tenants], and all artificers, as tailors, shoe-makers, carpenters, bricklayers, masons, etc...'. Yet, Sir Thomas points out, sometimes for lack of yeomen such people were given posts of churchwardens, inspectors of ale and constables. Dogberry and Verges in *Much Ado About Nothing* obviously belonged to this class.

ELIZABETHAN LONDON

Towards the end of the Middle Ages the richest citizens of London had become politically no less important than the greatest landowners among the nobility. In the Elizabethan period London reached enormous proportions both in size and importance. Its population rose from 70 000 in the beginning of the sixteenth century to 200 000 at its close. Nowadays this would not be considered very large, but, compared to the population of an average Elizabethan town, which was 5 000, this was an enormous figure. This increase in population reflects the enormous importance of the city at the time. London then became the centre of home and foreign trade. Visitors to the city were impressed by the amount of business transacted in it, the noise and bustle of its streets, the magnificent dress of its men and women and the number of palaces built along the Thames for the nobility and of stately houses and mansions in the city belonging to its aldermen and leading citizens.

A modern visitor to Elizabethan London, however, would be struck by the discrepancy between beauty and ugliness, grandeur and sordidness, which life in that city presented at once. This was, as it were, the outward expression of the paradox from which the substance of tragedy is derived. Apart from the intellectual and religious conceptions of life which emphasised the chasm between the angelic and beastly in man, on the plane of social every day living the huge gap separating the two sides of life could be seen and felt by the sensitive man. Side by side with the grand and costly palaces were the dirty rat-ridden streets. Along with the extravagance and fine costume went the constant fear of death in its most hideous shape, the plague, of which several detailed and harrowing descriptions have been preserved for us. Along the river Thames swans glided gracefully, but low in the London sky hovered birds of prey, crows, ravens and kites, which it was forbidden to kill because they 'devoured the filth of the streets'. The Thames itself was a scene of contradictions. As a modern author has put it, it was 'London's Sinister Street as well as its principal and most handsome thoroughfare'. Two or three thousand people crossed it daily in colourful barges, often singing songs or playing on their own musical instruments, in order to reach the theatres and other places of amusement on the south bank. Yet in the river they could easily see the corpses of the pirates and water thieves who had been hanged and deliberately left there until three tides had flooded over them and above their heads on the bridge they could see the skulls of those who had been beheaded for treason. Together with the pomp and ceremony and the respect for degree went violence and intriguing, the fall of princes, and the 'wheel of fortune' could be seen revolving by the Elizabethan Londoner no less visibly than during the Wars of the Roses. An obvious example was the career of the Earl of Essex, who after being the Queen's favourite and the people's hero, led a futile revolt against her, which only ended by his execution.

Life in Elizabethan London was a much more exciting, much more violent affair than it is in London today. The Elizabethan age was the great age of English seamen. People like Drake, Hawkins and Raleigh reflected the adventurous spirit of individualism and private enterprise, which was infectious at the time. Apart from the economic effect they had on the London merchants, their voyages became common topics of conversation among scholars, statesmen, merchants and adventurous youth alike. To their miraculous adventures in unknown lands we should relate the setting of *The Tempest*. In our study of the Elizabethans we must forget the current view of the quiet and reserved Englishman. Instead, we must imagine someone given to violent games and noisy modes of entertainment, like bear-baiting and cock-fighting. Commenting on the English, a foreign visitor to London wrote in 1598, 'They are vastly fond of great noises that fill the ear, such as the firing of cannon, drums and the ringing of bells'. Seen in relation to the life of the times the noise, with which Shakespeare's plays abound, is not really excessive. Duels and street brawls of the type we see in *Romeo and Juliet* were daily occurrences. In these brawls the London apprentices played a prominent part, especially as most of these apprentices, Stowe tells us, were 'often the children of gentlemen and persons of good quality', and in their spare time 'affected to go in costly attire and wear weapons and frequent schools of dancing, fencing and music'. They also flocked to the theatres, which were often the scenes of riots, a fact which caused their masters, no less than the puritans, to oppose the theatres. There was much cony-catching or swindling in London (as we find in *The Winter's Tale*), much thieving of the type we find in *Henry IV Part 1*, especially as merchants in those days travelled with large sums of money for purposes of business, since banks had not yet come into existence. Offenders were severely punished. A contemporary foreigner was told that 'above three hundred were hanged annually' and that hanging (which in the cases of the more serious offences included disembowelling) was considered more ignoble than beheading. Beheading was the punishment reserved for noblemen who had been convicted of high treason. Hanging took place at Tyburn (where Marble Arch stands now), while the scene of beheading was the Tower. Offenders about to be hanged were taken from their prisons to Tyburn on an open cart with a rope round their necks. The skulls of the beheaded noblemen were fixed to stakes and displayed on London Bridge. Death, bloody death, was a common sight. People flocked to watch scenes of hanging with the same zest as they saw spectacles of bear-baiting. On his way to The Globe Theatre Shakespeare could not avoid seeing such gory sights. Equally violent, but no less fascinating for the common man in Elizabethan London, were the occasional sights of the burning of witches and religious heretics, which took place also at Tyburn. It is not surprising then to find so many bloody spectacles in Shakespeare's plays.

Such was the London in which, during his career as a dramatist, Shakespeare lived, a city of contradictions, full of colour and gaiety, of song and dance and hope for the future, but not far off lurked death and violence, fear of the unknown and the inexplicable, of witches and the eclipses of the moon, and of the plague. Between these two extremes man lived out his short but full life, pulled in opposite directions, just as the Elizabethan world view pictured him.

4 Cosmology and Religion

In an essay entitled 'The Absence of Religion in Shakespeare', written at the turn of the century, the American philosopher and critic George Santayana complained that Shakespeare's world 'is only the world of human society', that 'the idea of cosmos eludes him' and that he 'depicts human life in all its richness and variety, but leaves that life without a setting and consequently without a meaning'. This view of Shakespeare was, in fact, for some time the prevalent and fashionable opinion until subsequent research and scholarship revealed that it is not entirely free from error. Shakespeare's plays are not religious drama in any sense of the term, nor does Shakespearean tragedy express a Christian view of life in which there is a definite answer to the questions raised about the destiny of man. Still they, no less than other serious plays of the Elizabethan age, do reflect, either directly or by implication, a more or less coherent picture of the universe. Without knowing something about that picture, which in its basic features is Christian, one is likely to fall into errors and misunderstandings concerning the poet's works. The plays themselves may not be Christian, but their framework often is. Shakespeare's characters do not live in a vacuum, and that is perhaps one reason why we feel that they are so convincing and real; they live in a particular society in which men's behaviour is judged by reference to certain standards and assumptions, some of which are obviously Christian. Some of these characters either exercise priestly functions themselves or stand for Christian values. Furthermore, the language of the plays is often charged with religious associations from which it derives some of its effectiveness. This does not mean that in order to appreciate Shakespeare one has to be a Christian. It only means that a knowledge of the Christian background of the plays is often helpful, and at times necessary. For instance, a play like *Macbeth* would lose part of its effect if the cosmic and religious setting in which it is placed was overlooked.

The externals of the Christian Church such as the hierarchical structure of the clergy have already been dealt with in the preceding chapter. We may now consider the Christianity of the Elizabethan view of man and the universe. This was basically medieval. As such it was eclectic in the sense that it tried to bring together and reconcile whatever branches of knowledge were available at the time. Some of the most important ingredients of this world view were of classical origin. In fact, the whole structure of the universe as conceived by the Elizabethan mind was, as it had been in the Middle Ages, based on classical foundations. For instance, the Elizabethan cosmology was still, in spite of the appearance of Copernicus, Ptolemaic, assuming the earth to be the stationary centre of the universe with the sun and stars revolving round it; the theory of the four elements and the conception of the 'Great Chain of Being' were Greek and the rationalism and stoicism were Greek and Roman. In a sense, then, part of what will be discussed here should belong to the next chapter dealing with the classical background. The reason for including all this material here is that the final picture made up of these classical elements had a specifically Christian meaning, in the Renaissance no less than in the Middle Ages.

Admittedly there were new elements introduced in sixteenth century England that justify the use of the term Renaissance. Besides, as we have seen in the previous chapter, the position of the clergy was altered considerably in the Tudor period; the leading government offices were secularised. Yet this must in no way lead us to believe that the Tudor or Elizabethan age was an essentially secular one. Unlike the Italian Renaissance which had a somewhat pagan tendency, the English Renaissance was strongly religious and ethical. After all, we must not forget that one of the results of the Reformation was that the King of England became also the head of the Church. Queen Elizabeth herself translated the Christian author Boethius. People's minds were then preoccupied with religious and theological issues, and that in a deep sense. In the Elizabethan period church attendance was made compulsory, and in the homilies that priests had to read to their congregations a comprehensive world picture is clearly and emphatically drawn.

In its broad outlines this picture is as follows: God in His perfection created the perfect universe in which absolute har-

mony prevailed; but motivated by pride the bad angels led by
Satan rebelled against God. Man was then created in God's image,
but unfortunately he succumbed to the temptation and ate of the
forbidden fruit. As a result the harmony of the universe was
disturbed. Man's fall introduced an element of corruption in the
divine order of the universe. This order, however, though now
not perfect, is still visible, and the situation is not altogether
hopeless, since Christ by means of the incarnation and atonement
for man's sins, through the act of crucifixion and resurrection,
has given man the hope of salvation. By the grace of God man can
be saved, but he should also lead a good life and even (where this
is possible) rise to a contemplation of God by means of studying
the manifestations of divine order in created things.

THE UNIVERSE

The Elizabethans' belief was that the created universe is sharply
divided into two most unequal parts. The smaller part is the
sublunary world; the world of time and change, of birth, repro-
duction and decay, of life and death, or as they often called it, the
world of mutability. This is the earth, which is at once the centre
of the universe and its lowest and crudest part. It is surrounded by
water, and above it are air and fire. Of all the four elements earth
is the basest and is followed in order of nobility by water, air and
fire. Fire, therefore, is the noblest element and is found next to the
sphere of the moon. The earth is in the form of a sphere and
around it revolve a number of concentric spheres, which form the
second and infinitely larger part of the universe. The moon is
the dividing line between the world of time and change and the
timeless and eternal world of the planets and stars. Shakespeare's
phrase 'beneath the visiting moon', for example, loses much of its
effect if divorced from this cosmic setting. Above the moon are
Mercury, Venus and the sun, Mars, Jupiter, Saturn, the fixed
stars, and then the sphere of *Primum Mobile* which is regulated by
the highest order of angels called Seraphs, and which set all the
spheres in motion, thereby producing a heavenly music, the
music of the spheres. This music cannot be heard by the 'sensual
ear' (see Lorenzo's words to Jessica in *The Merchant of Venice* V i

63–5) although man was able to hear it before the fall. Each of the spheres is directed by an order of angels or 'Intelligences'. God Himself was believed to reside, attended by the hosts of the angels, in the 'empyrean' region beyond the fixed stars.

According to the Elizabethans all created things were linked together and arranged in a fixed pattern or hierarchy, which was often thought of in terms of a ladder or chain—the great chain of being. The metaphor, says Dr Tillyard (in *The Elizabethan World Picture*, p. 23, Chatto and Windus, London, 1943)

> served to express the unimaginable plenitude of God's creation, its unfaltering order, and its ultimate unity. The chain stretched from the foot of God's throne to the meanest of inanimate objects. Every speck of creation was a link in the chain, and every link except those at the two extremities was simultaneously bigger and smaller than another: there could be no gap.

Between God and man the angels hold an intermediate position. Their nature is purely intellectual and their function is to act as God's messengers and to protect men—that is if we except those angels who fell from grace, and who are out to do mankind much harm.

Like the angels man possesses the faculty of reason, but whereas they are pure intelligence man also partakes of the nature of what is immediately below him, the beast. This is his place in the cosmic setting, a unique place, since he is the link between matter and spirit: below the angels and above the beast. Below man, who combines existence, life, feeling and understanding, are the animals, which have all these qualities except understanding, and below the animals are the plants, which possess existence and life but no sensitivity. At the bottom of the scale is mere existence without life, like metals. Because man combines within himself all the qualities of earthly existence he is often called the little world or microcosm.

Within each of these classes there is to be observed a rigid hierarchy, or as it is sometimes called 'degree' (for instance, by Shakespeare in the famous speech by Ulysses in *Troilus and Cressida* I iii 85ff.). Among the metals, for example, gold is higher in the scale of being than brass, the dolphin is placed above all the fish, the eagle above all the birds, the lion above all the beasts. In the world of vegetation the oak is considered nobler than all the other trees, and the rose is raised above all flowers. Among men the king or ruler is above his subjects. The father is the head of the family, and man is superior to woman. There is a hierarchy among the members of the human body: the head is raised above the rest, while the liver is the king of the lowest part and the heart the lord of the middle part. The same hierarchy is observed among the planets: the sun is raised in importance above all the other heavenly bodies. Even among the angels a rigid hierarchy prevailed, although there is no common agreement in the Elizabethan age on the names of the superior and inferior ranks. Among the names given to different orders we may mention: Seraphim, Cherubim, Thrones, Dominations, Virtues, Powers, Principalities, Archangels and Angels. Sometimes the Greek philosopher Plato's Ideas and Intelligences are added. Unlike the Middle Ages, the Elizabethan age tended to put the Archangels at the top of the angelic hierarchy. The Elizabethan conception of the universe is so integrated and unified that in it there are the most subtle relations of correspondence. For example, there is a relation of correspondence between the king among men, the sun among the planets, the lion among the beasts, the eagle among the birds and the rose among the flowers and so on. There is also the obvious correspondence between the macrocosm, the universe, and the microcosm, man. Besides there is a relation of sympathy between the various parts of the universe.

Such, in brief, is the picture of cosmic order which the average Elizabethan tacitly or consciously accepted. Through it he saw the whole of the universe in an integrated pattern, which was majestic and awe-inspiring. He also felt that he was not an outsider living in an indifferent universe, but that he had his place in its total pattern. But the pattern was sometimes precarious: the harmony of the created universe could only prevail as long as things remained in the place assigned to them in the scheme of things. Because of the sympathetic relations in the universe, if disorder occurred in any part of it, it was bound to have its repercussions on the whole. The Elizabethan was, therefore, sometimes haunted by feelings of insecurity and even vague metaphysical fear lest order should be ousted by chaos (which was struggling to find its way back through man's sin) whenever he saw any of the links forming the chain of being overstepping its proper station. On the other hand, by enabling man to see that whatever happened on earth was expressly part of a divine plan the pattern gave his life purpose and significance. Moreover, it did not necessarily lead to extreme pessimism. The earth, it is true, was the basest of the elements and it contained the dregs of the universe, but man was the lord of all earthly creatures, and after all he was created in God's image.

Besides, the details of that pattern, the individual links of which the great chain was constituted, and the infinite correspondences it contained, supplied the poets, and Shakespeare preeminently, with an endless fund of metaphor and imagery, which was at the same time more than just poetic imagery, because it was charged with a great collective emotional energy. Shakespeare often describes his kings in terms of the sun or the eagle or dolphin, and uses fire as an indication of nobility, and music as an expression of order and harmony both within and without. But perhaps the best example of Shakespeare's use of such details of world order is to be found in *Macbeth*. When Macbeth murders his king, the whole order, we are meant to understand, is upset. The whole of nature suffers from an upheaval as a result, and Macbeth's act has its cosmic reverberations. We learn this first from the choric commentary Shakespeare has given to Lennox. Describing the night on which King Duncan is murdered (although Lennox does not as yet know it), he says:

> The night has been unruly: where we lay,
> Our chimneys were blown down; and, as they say,
> Lamentings heard i'the air; strange screams of death,
> And prophesying with accents terrible
> Of dire combustion and confus'd events
> New hatch'd to the woeful time. The obscure bird
> Clamour'd the livelong night: some say the earth
> Was feverous and did shake.   (II iii 54–61)

But more explicitly is the reversal of natural order revealed in the dialogue between Ross and an Old Man. They also comment on the time of the murder:

Old man: Threescore and ten I can remember well;
   Within the volume of which time I have seen
   Hours dreadful and things strange, but this sore night
   Hath trifled former knowings.
Ross: Ah! good father,
   Thou seest, the heavens, as troubled with man's act,
   Threaten his bloody stage: by the clock 't is day,
   And yet dark night strangles the travelling lamp.
   Is't night's predominance, or the day's shame,
   That darkness does the face of earth entomb,
   When living light should kiss it?
Old Man: 'Tis unnatural.
   Even like the deed that's done. On Tuesday last,
   A falcon, towering in her pride of place,
   Was by a mousing owl hawk't at and kill'd.
Ross: And Duncan's horses,—a thing most strange and
                            certain,—
   Beauteous and swift, the minions of their race,
   Turn'd wild in nature, broke their stalls, flung out,
   Contending 'gainst obedience, as they would
   Make war with mankind.
Old Man: 'Tis said they eat each other.
Ross: They did so; to the amazement of mine eyes,
   That look'd upon't.   (II iv 1–20)

The details enumerated in this description are not just poetic
images or a mode of pathetic fallacy (that is, a poetic device
of making nature sympathise with man's feelings). To an
Elizabethan they are rather an indication that the whole order of
nature is upset. Degree has gone: the falcon, for instance, which is
the king of birds is killed by an inferior creature, the owl, just as
King Duncan is murdered by his subject and subordinate,
Macbeth. Similarly natural law has ceased to operate, and nature
has turned wild. Shakespeare, here, is obviously drawing upon a
body of common beliefs and assumptions. In fact, if we turn to the
source of the play we shall realise that what we have here is
something rather like the product of collective imagination: most
of the details themselves Shakespeare has derived from his
source. The two following extracts from Holinshed's *History of*

Scotland describe the effect of the murder, not of King Duncan, but of King Duffe:

> Holinshed, ii, *History of Scotland*, 151/1/12: For the space of six months together, after this heinous murder thus committed there appeared no sun by day, nor moon by night in any part of the realm, but still was the sky covered with continual clouds, and sometimes such outrageous winds arose, with lightenings and tempests, that the people were in great fear of present destruction.

> Holinshed, ii, *History of Scotland*, 152/1/9: Monstrous sights also that were seen within the Scottish kingdom that year were these: horses in Louthian, being of singular beauty and swiftness, did eat their own flesh, and would in no wise taste any other meat. . . . There was a sparhawk also strangled by an owl. Neither was it any less wonder that the sun, as before is said, was continually covered with clouds for six months space. But all men understood that the abominable murder of King Duffe was the cause hereof.

By mentioning such details Shakespeare not only heightens the effect of Macbeth's crime, but he also adds a religious dimension to the play, placing it in a cosmological and Christian context. The harmony of the universe is shown to be disturbed by Macbeth's crime, just as it was originally upset by Adam's fall. We are, therefore, meant to see Macbeth's yielding to the temptation as 'another fall of man'—a phrase which Shakespeare himself uses in connection with a similar act of treachery in another play (*Henry V* II ii 142).

MAN

By his fall man has rendered himself open to the influence of fortune, which in Elizabethan opinion takes the form of the stars working in conjunction with man's character. Because the question of the freedom of the will is of immediate relevance to drama, especially to tragedy, a word must be said about the Elizabethan conception of character or psychology. The Elizabethans believed that what decided the quality of a man, no less than that of a beast or an inanimate thing, was the proportions in which the four elements were mixed in him. If the proportions were right the product was more perfect and less easily subject to decay and corruption. For instance, in diamond the elements would be better mixed than in any other stone. At the end of *Julius Caesar*, when Antony wants to convey the idea of Brutus's excellence and nobility of character, he says that

> the elements
> So mix'd in him that Nature might stand up
> And say to all the world, 'This was a man!'   (V v 73–5)

The four elements of which man's body was made were obviously earth, water, air and fire, which were found in the food he ate. These were turned by the liver into the four humours — which were liquid substances possessing the same primary qualities of heat, cold, moisture and dryness as their corresponding elements. The earth was converted into melancholy (both being cold and dry); water into phlegm (both being cold and moist); air into blood (both being hot and moist) while fire was turned into choler (both were hot and dry). The humours produced a vital heat, called 'spirits', which was formed in the liver, then carried along the veins to the heart and subsequently to the brain, becoming refined and rarified at each stage. A man's character or 'temperament' or 'complexion' became melancholic, phlegmatic, sanguine or choleric according to the prevalence of any of these humours in his constitution. When any of them, however, was found in excess this might lead to violent passion and weakness before temptation and so probably to sin. Besides, if any of the humours went bad, then the result was 'melancholy' in the narrow Elizabethan sense of the word, indicating some abnormality in the character.

Each of the four types of temperament was distinguished by certain physical and moral characteristics. The 'sanguine' man was of medium height and had soft smooth skin, a handsome face and golden or auburn hair. In character he was brave, generous, merry, amorous and fond of food and drink. As examples of this type among Shakespeare's characters we may mention Antony in *Antony and Cleopatra* and in some respects Sir Toby Belch in

Twelfth Night. The choleric man was tall with dark hair, brown skin and 'dark piercing eyes'; he was generally rash, warlike, ambitious and arrogant. To such a type would belong Coriolanus, Hotspur in *Henry IV* and Fluellen in *Henry V*. In appearance the phlegmatic tended to be short and rather fat; he would have white skin, long, lank hair of a dull colour and dull watery eyes. In character he was slow, stupid, lazy and cowardly. A perfect example of this type is Sir Andrew Aguecheek in *Twelfth Night* (although the stage tradition tends to portray him as thin). As for the melancholic he was by far the most complex of all the types in Elizabethan psychology. He tended to be slow and heavy in movement, taciturn, unsociable, suspicious, cruel in revenge and to suffer from insomnia and bad dreams, unnecessary fears and anxieties. Often he was an intellectual who shunned the company of men and sought solitude. Among the Shakespearean characters that would be easily identified by the Elizabethan audience as either melancolics or based on the melancholy temperament would be Antonio in *The Merchant of Venice*, Jacques in *As You Like It*, Timon of Athens and Hamlet. For a fuller treatment of this point the reader may turn to J. B. Bamborough's excellent book *The Little World of Man* (Longmans, Green & Co., London, 1952).

As is clear, there is a good deal of implicit determinism in this physiological theory of character. As Hamlet himself says (I iv 25), nobody can be held responsible for the particular mixture of humours with which he is born. Besides, planetary influences were usually involved in the predominance of the humours. Men born under different planets tended to have particular conditions of the body and therefore of the mind. Men born under Jupiter tended to be handsome, fair, honest and generous, while those born under Mars were inclined to be tall and thin and tended to be rebellious, revengeful and 'fiery'. Saturn made for prudence and the pursuit of learning, but those born under its evil aspect were often ugly and slow and suffered from melancholy. The effect of Venus was to make men fair, graceful, voluptuous and to inspire in them a love of music and singing. Mercury, on the other hand, made men subtle, wise and eloquent. The sun made people handsome, cheerful, truthful and religious. As for the moon it governed the humours of the body and had a direct influence on the brain. In fact, the influence of the other planets was directly related to the position of the moon, which was considered the chief agent of change in the 'sublunary' world. As a rule the stars were constantly exercising their influence, whether at the moment a man was born, or later on at crucial points in his life. The rule of the world beneath the moon was change or mutability, and the most obvious image in which this mutability was conceived, the Wheel of Fortune, is only too well known in Elizabethan literature, especially in the drama.

The influence of the stars, however, must not be overrated. The Elizabethans still believed in the freedom of man's will. Admittedly the stars might give a man a certain disposition, for, after all, the whole of the universe was essentially interrelated, and it was inconceivable that the heavenly bodies should have no effect whatever upon man. By affecting the air, for instance, by increasing heat and dryness, the stars too might affect the bodies of men and consequently their minds. In this respect their power was unavoidable. But in the last analysis man was partly the master of his own fate. Only a weak man would fail to control the effect of the stars or would succumb to their power. After all, the belief in the power of the stars was not always a matter of superstition: it was argued by some that the planets were created to do what was only good, and their opposite effect was really the result of man's fall, which disturbed the harmony of the universe. In exercising their influence over man they were only obeying God's orders. Ultimately, therefore, what they did was part of the overall divine plan. Nevertheless, man could resist and mitigate their influence and rise above fortune by means of reason. It was only over beasts that the influence of the stars was of necessity supreme.

According to the Elizabethans, reason, which is the divine element in man's nature, the element that distinguishes him from the beasts and makes him more akin to God and the angels, consists of two aspects: the understanding or wit, and the will. Unlike the angels, man's intelligence and will are of necessity imperfect. Whereas the angels know all they are capable of knowing and their knowledge is intuitive, man starts from a state of ignorance and has to learn about God, the world of created things and himself, and that in the slow and painful discursive method. And the fall has impaired man's power of understanding, with the result that he is now only too easily subject to the illusion of the senses, and he often finds the act of thinking and learning in itself a rather painful process. Similarly, the fall has corrupted man's will. Whereas the angels only will that which accords with the will of God, man often acts against his better judgment, and follows the call of his instincts and passion against the dictates of his reason, thereby 'abandoning the dignity of his proper nature' and behaving like a beast. Not that the Elizabethans preached complete absence or denial of passion. They did indeed recognise it, but they recommended keeping it strictly under control. What was invoked was the rule of the golden mean and of moderation. What Hamlet admires in Horatio's character is that his 'blood and judgment are so well co-mingled'.

The struggle between blood and judgment, passion and reason, which lies at the heart of Shakespearean tragedy, had therefore obvious religious foundations. It arose from man's position between the angels and the beasts and from his being subject to the conflicting demands both worlds make on him. In this predicament what man should do was perfectly clear to the Elizabethans, and here the classical and Christian traditions most noticeably meet. Christianity as Saint Paul taught it, and as it was usually understood by Protestant England, preached primarily the victory of the spirit (or reason) over the flesh, just as Plato had previously taught that man's higher part, reason, should subjugate his baser passions. The vast contrast between what man is capable of being, if he allows reason to guide his life, and what he sometimes is like, when he gives in to his passion, forms one of the basic themes of Shakespearean tragedy. When Hamlet therefore says

> What a piece of work is a man: how noble in reason; how infinite in faculty; in form and moving how express and admirable; in action how like an angel; in apprehension how like a god; the beauty of the world, the paragon of animals
>
> (II ii 307–11)

he is really describing both the state of man before the fall and what he is still capable of becoming. Yet thinking of what man actually is now, he describes him as 'this quintessence of dust' and he likens the inhabited world to 'an unweeded garden' possessed merely by 'things rank and gross'.

To assert his kinship to the angel, therefore, to free himself from the domination of the stars and to rise above the buffets and blows of fortune, man must never let his 'god-like reason' 'fust' in him 'unused'. But to make it possible for reason to guide him it is imperative that he should know himself, and so keep a constant watch on himself in case any of his passions should suddenly break loose. In *King Lear* Shakespeare has powerfully illustrated the great difficulty of self-knowledge, while in *Othello* he has portrayed the disastrous effect of passion let loose. As for the possibility of self-mastery he has given us a dramatic presentation of it in *The Tempest*, a play which in many ways can be regarded as illustrative of man's proper position in the scale of being.

We may now turn from the general Christian view of the universe, which is the background of Shakespeare's plays, to the more specific use of, and allusion to, themes and incidents from the Bible. It is here that the reader unacquainted with Christianity and the Scripture finds the greatest difficulty. Such a reader can readily grasp the general features of the world picture expressed or assumed in the plays, but the particular emotional effect of an allusion to an incident from the Scriptures, or of the insertion of a Biblical phrase in a speech, will inevitably be lost on him. Yet the plays abound in such echoes and allusions, just as in the Islamic tradition, if one may bring in an analogy from another culture, Arabic secular literature abounds in allusions to the *Koran*.

There is no general agreement among scholars on the extent of Shakespeare's knowledge of the Bible, although it is certain that he read certain parts of it. He must have read at least the books of *Genesis* and *Job*, and his knowledge of the *Psalms* was extensive, since there is hardly a single play of his in which we do not find quotations from the *Psalms*. The Bible was the most widely read book in Shakespeare's time. There were already three translations of it available for him, known respectively as the Great Bible (1539), the Geneva Bible (1560) and the Bishops' Bible (1568), King James' Authorized Version which was completed in 1611 being too late for him to use. Even assuming that he did not read the Bible himself he must have heard it read in church. The homilies and sermons he heard contained passages from the Bible, and indeed even the secular literature of the time, some of which Shakespeare must have read, was full of biblical echoes and phrases. Besides, there was the Prayer Book from which Shakespeare quoted often in the plays. In short, in an age when biblical subjects were much discussed and when there was a deep and general interest in religion it was impossible for an intelligent man like Shakespeare not to acquire the biblical knowledge which is revealed in his writings. Furthermore, Shakespeare's use of the Bible in his plays presupposes the existence in his audience too of a certain degree of familiarity with biblical themes and language.

Shakespeare's use of the Bible ranges from the casual verbal echo to the overt allusion to a particular personage, episode or parable in the Scripture, from the employment of a scriptural text as a means of characterisation to the use of a biblical idea as an underlying theme for a play. He even gives one of his plays, *Measure for Measure*, a title which is based on a sentence from the Bible: Matthew vii 2, 'and with what measure ye mete, it shall be measured to you again*'. By echoing, consciously or unconsciously, the language of the Bible Shakespeare lent a certain dignity to his own language, heightening its effect on his audience, or at least that large section of his audience familiar with the original. As a means of characterisation the use of Biblical quotation was a convenient device to suggest scholarship, learning and reflection in the speaker. Shakespeare's audience knew parts of their Bible, and they also knew that it was a subject of learned commentary. Hearing a character on the stage, such as Prince Hamlet, for instance, quoting from, or referring to, the Bible, they would immediately identify him as a learned scholar. Shakespeare also shows Richard of Gloucester trying to impress the Mayor and Citizens of London with his devotion and lack of interest in worldly affairs by means of frequent quotation from the Scripture.

When Hamlet describes his hands as 'these pickers and stealers'

---

* It is useful to quote the whole passage because it forms an admirable comment on the play, especially on the behaviour of Angelo: 'Judge not, that ye be not judged. For with what judgment ye judge, ye shall be judged: and with what measure ye mete, it shall be measured to you again. And why beholdest thou the mote that is in thy brother's eye, but considerest not the beam that is in thine own eye? Or how wilt thou say to thy brother, let me pull out the mote out of thine eye, and, behold, a beam is in thine own eye? Thou hypocrite, first cast out the beam out of thine own eye; and then shalt thou see clearly to cast out the mote out of thy brother's eye.' (Matthew, vii 1–5). The quotations here are from the 1611 English translation of the Bible.

(III ii 321) he is obviously referring to the phrase in the Anglican Catechism, which every Elizabethan knew by heart, 'to keep my hands from picking and stealing'. This is an example of allusion to the Prayer Book, but allusions to the Bible are numerous. Here I shall only mention very few examples. When Hamlet sees his uncle at prayer he refrains from killing him and decides to put off his vengeance until he catches him in an act 'which has no relish of salvation in it'. The reason he gives is that his uncle had not given his father the chance to repent when he murdered him, or as he puts it:

> He took my father grossly, full of bread,
> With all his crimes broad blown, as flush as May
> (III iii 80–1)

The force of the expression 'full of bread' arises from its biblical association, for it is derived from the biblical phrase 'fulness of bread' (Ezekiel xvi 49), indicating sin and indulgence in earthly pleasures. Othello's words just before he murders his wife:

> This sorrow's heavenly,
> It strikes where it doth love   (V ii 21–2)

cannot be understood without reference to the sentence from the Bible 'Whom the Lord loveth he chasteneth' (Hebrews xii 6). Apart from enforcing the ambivalent nature of Othello's feelings towards Desdemona, the religious allusion here enhances the ritualistic quality of Othello's murder and reveals his attitude to the murder which he regards in a ghastly way more as a sacrifice than as a murder or an act of vengeance. Again when Hamlet says 'there is special providence in the fall of a sparrow' (V ii 219–20) he is alluding to the following: 'Are not two sparrows sold for a farthing, and one of them shall not fall on the ground without your Father' (Matthew x 29). The quotation from the New Testament reflects the change that occurred in Hamlet's character after his return to Denmark, from his earlier restlessness and constant rebellion against his destiny ('O cursed spite That ever I was born to set it right') to a calm and almost resigned acceptance of his fate. In *Hamlet*, again, Claudius's soliloquy (III iii 36 ff.) opens with the words

> O! my offence is rank, it smells to heaven;
> It hath the primal eldest curse upon't;
> A brother's murder

which refer to Cain's murder of his brother Abel. In the course of the soliloquy he says,

> What if this curs'd hand
> Were thicker than itself with brother's blood,
> Is there not rain enough in the sweet heavens
> To wash it white as snow?

To an Elizabethan these words would recall the biblical text, 'Though your sins be as scarlet they shall be as white as snow,' (Isaiah i 18). In *Richard III* the words 'Woe to the land that's govern'd by a child' (II iii 11) are to the Elizabethan audience a reminder of the Biblical 'Woe to thee, O land, when thy king is a child' (Ecclesiastes x 16). Similarly in *Troilus and Cressida* the words 'A generation of Vipers' (III i 137) echo 'O generation of vipers' (Matthew iii 7). In *Measure for Measure* Claudio's words

> To sue to live, I find I seek to die,
> And, seeking death, I find life   (III i 42–3)

are a paraphrase of 'For whosoever will save his life, shall lose it: again, whosoever will lose his life for my sake, shall find it' (Matthew xvi 25).

But to enable the reader to realise how profoundly influenced by the Bible Shakespeare's language was, it is perhaps best to consider a familiar passage from one of his best known plays, *Macbeth*. The passage is Macbeth's famous soliloquy, which we have already quoted in an earlier chapter in order to illustrate the peculiar manner in which Shakespeare's imagery works:

> To-morrow, and to-morrow, and to-morrow,
> Creeps in this petty pace from day to day,
> To the last syllable of recorded time;
> And all our yesterdays have lighted fools
> The way to dusty death. Out, out, brief candle!
> Life's but a walking shadow, a poor player

> That struts and frets his hour upon the stage,
> And then is heard no more; it is a tale
> Told by an idiot, full of sound and fury,
> Signifying nothing.   (V v 19–28)

No less than four clear biblical ideas are alluded to in this passage. 'The way to dusty death' refers both to the phrase 'dust to dust' which occurs in the Book of Common Prayer, and to the sentence from the *Psalms* 'and thou hast brought me into the dust of death' (Psalms xxii 15). 'Out, out, brief candle!' is suggested by the sentence from *Job* (xviii 6) 'and his candle shall be put out with him'. Similarly, 'Life's but a walking shadow' echoes the sentence from the *Psalms* 'Man is like to vanity: his days are as a shadow that passeth away.' (Psalms cxliv 4) and 'Surely every man walketh in a vain shew' (Psalms xxxix 6). 'It is a tale Told by an idiot,' puts us in mind of those words from the *Psalms* 'we spend our years, as a tale that is told' (Psalms xc 9). Finally one cannot deny the possible influence upon the mood of the whole passage of these words from *Job*, 'For we are but of yesterday, and know nothing, because our days upon earth are a shadow' (viii 9). This example may perhaps suffice to show how Shakespeare's style is saturated with biblical language and thought.

In spite of the abundance of biblical allusions in all of them, the plays vary considerably in the number of references and quotations they contain. In this respect it is perhaps not surprising to find that a play such as *Measure for Measure*, which beside deriving its title from the Bible lends itself easily to a Christian interpretation, has more biblical allusions than any other play by Shakespeare. Occasionally Shakespeare expresses himself in the explicit language of orthodox Christianity. For instance in *Richard III* we read:

> as you hope to have redemption
> By Christ's dear blood shed for our grievous sins
>
> > (I iv 194–5)

or in the same play.

> and defac'd
> The precious image of our dear Redeemer   (II i 123–4)

or in *Henry IV Part I:*

> those holy fields
> Over whose acres walk'd those blessed feet
> Which fourteen hundred years ago were nail'd
> For our advantage on the bitter cross   (I i 24–7)

Christ is mentioned by name in *Henry VI Parts 1 and 2*, in *Richard III* and *Richard II*, in *Henry IV Part 1* and in *Henry V*. He is also referred to as 'My Redeemer' in *Richard III*, as 'Our Saviour' in *Hamlet* and as 'Blessed Mary's Son' in *Richard II*. But as a result of the act passed in 1605 forbidding the profane use on the stage of the name of God, or Jesus Christ or the Holy Ghost or the Holy Trinity, we find that Shakespeare used the words 'Heaven' or 'Jove' instead of God. He also used the expressions 'King of Heaven', 'King of kings', 'High All-Seer', 'Lord of Hosts', 'The Eternal', 'the Highest' and 'the Everlasting'. (See Richard Noble, *Shakespeare's Biblical Knowledge*, SPCK, London, 1935.)

There are many characters and incidents from the Scripture alluded to in Shakespeare's plays. A few of them, the ones that appear frequently in his works, will be discussed. Firstly there is the Fall of Man, the story of which is narrated mainly in *Genesis*, which Shakespeare knew intimately. Adam was the first man whom God created of dust and set to mind the garden of Eden. In Eden he lived with Eve, the mother of mankind, in a state of innocence until the devil, assuming the shape of a serpent, tempted her and she ate of the forbidden fruit (Satan or the devil is alluded to in the plays in a number of different ways: he is called Beelzebub, Lucifer, the Prince of darkness, Prince of this world). At the instigation of Eve, Adam transgressed, both thereby losing their innocence. They were banished from Eden and condemned to work and suffer on earth. Their first born, Cain, who was a tiller of the ground, slew his brother Abel, a keeper of sheep, because the latter's sacrifices were more acceptable to God. Cain was, therefore, cursed, banished and marked. In religious drama Cain is said to have been represented as having a yellow beard. There is also the story of the Flood which God brought about to destroy mankind and all living things on earth, because of their 'wickedness', and the Ark which He commanded the good patriarch Noah to build to save himself, his wife and children and two of every living thing. Noah was a popular figure in medieval religious drama. Another biblical figure made popular because a ballad had been written about him is Jephah or Jephthah who was Judge of Israel. Before setting out to fight the Ammonites he vowed that if he had the victory he would sacrifice the first living creature 'that cometh out of the doors of my house against me, when I come in peace from the children of Ammon'. It so happened that what he first saw on his victorious return from the wars was his only daughter who had come dancing out of the door to greet her father, so he slew her. Jephthah is referred to twice by Shakespeare, in *Henry VI Part 3* and in *Hamlet*. A third figure from the Bible, who was even better known because of his frequent appearance in religious drama, was Herod, the bloodthirsty king of Judea, who, when told about the infant Christ who was going to be king of the Jews, ordered all the male infants round about Bethlehem to be slaughtered. In the mystery plays he was represented as a raging tyrant, and he is mentioned at least four times by Shakespeare, in *Henry V*, *Merry Wives of Windsor*, *Hamlet* and *Antony and Cleopatra*.

Of the parables in the Gospels two deserve to be mentioned because of the frequent allusion to them in Shakespeare's plays: the parable of the Prodigal Son and that of Dives and Lazarus. The first is referred to in at least eight plays. It is the parable used by Christ to illustrate that Heaven rejoices more over the repentance of one sinner than 'over ninety and nine just persons, which need no repentance'. The story, briefly, is that of a man who had two sons. The 'younger' or the 'prodigal' asked his father to give him his portion of wealth, 'took his journey into a far country' where he wasted his fortune 'with riotous living'. After having suffered much through poverty, especially during a famine, he repented his sins and decided to return home from his wanderings. There were celebrations and festivities to welcome his return, and at his father's command the fatted calf was killed for him, much to the annoyance of the more responsible brother who complained that he had been serving his father obediently for a good many years without the father giving him even a kid. The father replied, saying that 'it was meet that we should make merry, and be glad: for this thy brother was dead, and is alive again; was lost, and is found'. The other parable is that of Dives or the rich man and Lazarus the beggar, indicating the reversal of fortune in the next world. Dives was a rich man 'clothed in purple and fine linen' who 'fared sumptuously every day' (in pictures he was usually represented as feasting), while at his gate lived Lazarus, a beggar full of sores which the dogs came and licked and 'desiring to be fed with the crumbs which fell from the rich man's table'. When both died Lazarus 'was carried by the angels into Abraham's bosom' (that is, the abode of the blessed), but Dives went to hell, where he was tormented by flames and desired in vain to have his tongue cooled, while all the time being able to see 'Abraham afar off, and Lazarus in his bosom'.

The two major figures in the life of Christ who are mentioned or referred to a number of times by Shakespeare are Judas Iscariot who betrayed Christ by kissing him and who in painting and tapestry was represented with red hair. According to tradition he hanged himself on an elder tree. He is referred to in *Henry VI Part 3*, *Love's Labour's Lost*, *Richard II*, *As You Like It* and *The Winter's Tale*. The other figure is Pontius Pilate, the Roman governor of Judaea, who washed his hands to signify that he was innocent of Christ's blood, although he still delivered him to be crucified. The field of Golgotha, which means the place of the skull and was the scene of the crucifixion, is mentioned in two plays, *Richard II* and *Macbeth*.

Apart from the general Elizabethan world picture and the particular biblical echoes and allusions to incidents and figures from the Bible there are a number of priests, parsons and higher clergymen among the characters of Shakespeare's plays. Of the higher strata of clergymen, such as cardinals, archbishops and bishops, a word has already been said in the preceding chapter. The lower strata, both Papist and Protestant, are amply represented in the plays. There are two sketches of friars, of whom one is much more than a mere sketch, Friar Laurence in *Romeo and Juliet* and Friar Francis in *Much Ado About Nothing*. There are plenty of parsons or parish priests: the curates, Sir Nathaniel in *Love's Labour's Lost* and Sir Topas in *Twelfth Night*, the vicar Sir Oliver Martext in *As You Like It* and the parson Sir Hugh Evans in *Merry Wives of Windsor*. The title 'Sir' here is, of course, not an indication of knighthood, but a translation of the Latin title 'Dominus' which was originally given to clergymen who obtained the degree of Bachelor of Arts, but later 'came to be applied especially to the old-fashioned or ignorant priest who could only read the services and was not able to preach'. There are also two superb portraits of 'puritans' in Shakespeare's works, the exquisitely comic character of Malvolio in *Twelfth Night* and the almost tragic figure of Angelo in *Measure for Measure*. What Shakespeare attacks in puritanism is its hypocrisy and too rigid morality which condemns the simple and innocent pleasures of life or its 'cake and ale', to use Sir Toby Belch's words in *Twelfth Night.*

Christianity also influenced and helped to define the form of Shakespearean drama. The connection between Christianity and English drama, or drama in Western Europe in general, was a close one for a long time. The subject belongs properly to the history of drama, rather than to an introduction to Shakespeare. However, since certain aspects of the structure of Shakespearean drama can only be explained and indeed appreciated in the light of the development of English drama (for instance, the form of Shakespeare's history plays and in some respects the form of the romances or the last plays) a very brief historical account is given here. The beginnings of drama in the Middle Ages are to be found in religious ceremonies. Apart from the fact that the mass, which is the basic religious service in the Christian world, contains an element of drama, in the early Middle Ages the Church decided to educate the largely illiterate congregation by giving them a dramatic representation of the important incidents of the Christian faith on certain occasions like the nativity or birth of Jesus, and Easter when Christ rose from the tomb. These semi-dramatic additions to the liturgy of the church, which are called the 'Tropes', later developed into the 'Mysteries' in which detailed representations of the main events in the life of Christ from the Bible were given first outside the church by clergymen, and subsequently in the market place by members of the various guilds. Examples of the events dramatised are the creation of the angels, the fall of Lucifer, the creation of man and the garden of Eden, the fall of man, the flood and Noah's ark, the story of Abraham's sacrifice of his son, Isaac, the birth of Christ, the shepherds who worshipped the infant Jesus in the manger, Herod and the three kings (or wise men) who came to adore and to give their offerings to the infant Jesus, Herod's order of the massacre of the innocents (children), Jesus's trial before Pilate, Jesus's crucifixion and ascension. The representation of these events did not always follow faithfully the biblical narrative: presumably in order to keep up the interest of their audience the authors of these dramatic pieces occasionally added lighter and more mundane material to liven up their text. The best known examples are the comic altercations between Noah and his shrewish wife who would not join her husband in the ark and preferred the company of her friends, the gossips. Here we find the origin of the admixture of seriousness and levity which is to characterise Shakespearean and most Elizabethan drama. Even more significant is the theme of Mak, the shepherd thief, in the second Shepherds' Play (in the Wakefield Cycle of Mysteries). The play consists of two parts. In the first and much longer part the shepherds assemble, talk about familiar every day matters, grumble about their nagging wives, their low wages and the high taxes they have to pay, then they fall asleep. During their sleep Mak stealthily gets up, steals a sheep, takes it to his cottage where with the help of his wife he dresses it as a baby, puts it in a cradle, then goes back to his companions in the field and pretends to be fast asleep. The theft, however, is discovered with hilarious effect; when searching Mak's cottage for the stolen sheep one of the shepherds, who wants to give the baby a present of sixpence, notices that it has 'a long snout'. In the second part of the play an angel appears to the shepherds while they are guarding their flock to announce to them the birth of Jesus and bids them to go and see him in the crib. Guided by a brilliant star they go to Bethlehem and find the child in the manger with Mary kneeling beside him. They adore the baby Jesus and offer him little presents. The parallelism between the comic and serious parts of this simple play is obvious. In fact, we find here in a crude way the ironic relation between plot and subplot which we shall find in a more subtle and sophisticated form in some of Shakespeare's plays. Although out of the comic and realistic elements of such performances emerged the 'Interludes', which were crude comic and satirical sketches aimed at religious or political instruction, the mystery plays, whether they dealt with the life of Jesus or with the lives of saints like *Mary Magdalene*, remained on the whole fraught with comic elements. The mystery plays dealing with the lives of saints, or as they are sometimes called the 'Miracles', were not so popular in England as they were on the continent, especially Italy. But they still exercised an effect on the form of

Shakespeare's last plays, although in an indirect way.

Alongside the Mysteries and Miracles grew the 'Moralities', which portrayed in an allegorical form the struggle between good and evil for the control of man's soul. In such plays human attributes are externalised and personified, so their characters are really personified abstractions like Beauty, Wisdom and Good Deeds. One of the stock characters in most morality plays is the comic figure Vice which appears riding on the Devil's back and belabouring him with a wooden dagger (compare with Hamlet's description of his uncle as 'vice of kings' III iv 98); it is the ancestor of the riotous 'clown' in Elizabethan drama. Gradually these plays dealt with philosophical and political themes instead of religious instruction, and the abstractions became historical figures. Although their themes became more secular the plays retained much of their original form. Morality plays were still popular in Shakespeare's life time and they had a considerable influence on the form of his history plays. The exact nature of that influence will be explained in the course of the discussion of the history plays. Suffice it to say here that Christianity influenced not only the ideas and themes of Shakespearean drama, but also its form. The other considerable influence, which is of no less importance, is the classical influence, and this will be the subject of our next chapter.

5 The Classical Background

The age of Shakespeare is traditionally regarded as marking the full flowering of the English Renaissance. The term Renaissance means 'rebirth', and it refers to the revival of interest in, or the rediscovery of , the classics, the works of the ancient Greek and Roman authors. At one time people believed that the Middle Ages were 'dark', and that the transition from them to the Renaissance was abrupt and spectacular. Later opinion, however, has swung almost to the opposite extreme, so much so that some twenty years ago one scholar gave his book the title, *The English Renaissance, Fact or Fiction?*

It is now proved beyond any doubt that classical learning was not entirely of Renaissance origin, and that Renaissance humanism was a continuation of the Christian humanism of the Middle Ages, which had its roots in the early attempts made by the Church Fathers to bring together Christianity and the wisdom and learning of the ancient world. The opposition of the Church to classical literature did not last long, for it soon became apparent that practical considerations necessitated the inclusion of Latin authors in the medieval school curriculum. Classical literature was allegorically interpreted and Christian truth was found to lie underneath its attractive fabling. Because of the ethical tone of his writings the poet Virgil became a text book: his fourth eclogue was taken to prophesy the coming of the Messiah, and the whole of his epic, the *Aeneid*, was construed to represent the pilgrimage of the soul through life. Next to Virgil came Ovid, whose tales, however sensuous and pagan they might be, were made to yield the desired moral and religious lessons. Furthermore, Thomas Aquinas tried to reconcile Christianity and Aristotle. Much of the classical tradition was, therefore, passed on to the Renaissance as part of the Christian medieval heritage. For instance, the rationalism which was the prominent feature of the Thomist synthesis (of Christianity and Aristotle) may have lost its rigorously logical nature in the Renaissance, but as a guiding principle, both in philosophy and in ethics, reason reigned supreme in the Elizabethan view of world order. The Elizabethans believed that fundamentally order governs the cosmos, society and the individual human soul, that this order is rational and that it is a manifestation of divine law. To this philosophy of rational order, which is necessary for the understanding of Shakespeare's plays, various classical authors contributed their share.

Far from being a sudden phenomenon the Renaissance of the fifteenth and sixteenth centuries was, in fact, a culmination of a slow movement that gathered speed as a result of a number of factors. Not the least important of these factors was the invention of printing, which helped to spread knowledge of Greek and Latin manuscripts. Consequently, more and better equipped scholars appeared who produced reliable editions of ancient texts. More authors were now read, and works which had been only partially known and read in selections in the Middle Ages could now be read in their entirety. In England, as elsewhere, the need to make classical wisdom accessible to the unlearned reader was keenly felt, with the result that a large number of translators rendered much of the classical heritage into the English language. For instance, at least 35 classical works, mainly moral and philosophical, by such authors as Aristotle, Cicero and Seneca, were translated into English in the second quarter of the sixteenth century, and during the second half of the century we find no less than 140 translations of works covering a wide range of subjects: history, science, rhetoric, fiction, drama and poetry. (See Douglas Bush, *Mythology and the Renaissance Tradition in English Poetry*, pp. 27–8, the University of Minnesota Press, Minneapolis, 1932.) Authors like Ovid, Virgil, Seneca and Plutarch became available in English. The Renaissance authors had a great respect for the ancients, whose authority they invoked on every occasion, and whose works they regarded as models of good writing and as the storehouse of the wisdom of man.

When Shakespeare went to school Latin was considered, quite naturally, the language of learning. The question of the extent of Shakespeare's knowledge of the classics has been hotly disputed ever since Ben Jonson wrote of his 'little Latin and less Greek', and even now we cannot say that it has been settled once and for all. Some scholars claim that he had a wide and first-hand acquaintance with the classics, while others argue, more convincingly perhaps, that most of his classical knowledge was derived from translations. The object of this chapter is not to establish Shakespeare's debt to classical authors, but to try to explain the necessary classical background of Shakespeare's works, especially to a reader of whose education the classical tradition may not have formed a part. There are many references in Shakespeare's works to names from classical antiquity, and just as many mythological allusions. Shakespeare's two narrative poems deal with Greek and Latin subjects. Besides, several of his plays are about Greek and Roman historical personages, and one of them takes a Latin play for its model.

It is perhaps in the matter of classical mythology, the traditional stories about the 'heroic' age of Greece, that the student needs help most. Like biblical references classical allusions are charged with emotional associations which a reader brought up in a different culture is likely to miss. They may even tend to impede the flow of his reading of the text. Here are a few well-known examples from plays written in different periods of Shakespeare's career:

> *Lorenzo*: The moon shines bright: in such a night as this,
>   When the sweet wind did gently kiss the trees
>   And they did make no noise, in such a night
>   Troilus methinks mounted the Trojan walls,
>   And sigh'd his soul towards the Grecian tents,
>   Where Cressid lay that night.
> *Jessica*:   In such a night
>   Did Thisbe fearfully o'ertrip the dew,
>   And saw the lion's shadow ere himself,
>   And ran dismay'd away.
> *Lorenzo*:   In such a night
>   Stood Dido with a willow in her hand
>   Upon the wild sea-banks, and waft her love
>   To come again to Carthage.
> *Jessica*:   In such a night
>   Medea gather'd the enchanted herbs
>   That did renew old Aeson.   (*The Merchant of Venice* V i 1–14)

> *Falstaff*: When thou art king, let not us that are squires of the
>   night's body be called thieves of the day's beauty: let us be

Diana's foresters, gentlemen of the shade, minions of the
moon; and let men say, we be men of good government,
being governed as the sea is, by our noble and chaste mistress
of the moon, under whose countenance we steal.

(*Henry IV Part 1* I ii 23ff.)

Hamlet: That it should come to this!
  But two months dead: nay, not so much, not two:
  So excellent a king; that was, to this,
  Hyperion to a satyr; so loving to my mother
  That he might not beteem the winds of heaven
  Visit her face too roughly. Heaven and earth!
  Must I remember? Why, she would hang on him,
  As if increase of appetite had grown
  By what it fed on; and yet, within a month,
  Let me not think on't: Frailty, thy name is woman!
  A little month; or ere those shoes were old
  With which she follow'd my poor father's body,
  Like Niobe, all tears; why she, even she,—
  O God! a beast, that wants discourse of reason,
  Would have mourn'd longer,—married with mine uncle,
  My father's brother, but no more like my father
  Than I to Hercules: (*Hamlet* I ii 137ff.)

Hamlet: Look here, upon this picture, and on this;
  The counterfeit presentment of two brothers.
  See, what a grace was seated on this brow;
  Hyperion's curls, the front of Jove himself,
  An eye like Mars, to threaten and command,
  A station like the herald Mercury
  New lighted on a heaven-kissing hill . . . (*Hamlet* III iv 53ff.)

Perdita: Now, my fair'st friend,
  I would I had some flower's o'the spring that might
  Become your time of day; and yours, and yours,
  That wear upon your virgin branches yet
  Your maidenheads growing: O Proserpina!
  For the flowers now that frighted thou let'st fall
  From Dis's waggon! daffodils,
  That come before the swallow dares, and take

> The winds of March with beauty; violets dim,
> But sweeter than the lids of Juno's eyes
> Or Cytherea's breath; pale prim-roses,
> That die unmarried, ere they can behold
> Bright Phoebus in his strength, a malady
> Most incident to maids;   (*The Winter's Tale* IV iii 112ff.)

In these instances we find Shakespeare using classical mythology for tragic, comic or romance purposes. Instead of producing the desired effect these allusions only obstruct the reader's course, unless he happens to be familiar with them. Yet the part mythological allusions play in Shakespeare's works is considerable. It is true that they are most abundant and elaborate in his early work, where they sometimes possess little or no poetic or dramatic value, but are rather of the nature of decoration or ornament, and reveal the young poet's desire to impress and establish contact with the more learned section of his audience. Besides, generally there are more of them in the early comedies than in the mature tragedies. For instance, according to one scholar, R. K. Root (*Classical Mythology in Shakespeare*, p. 12, H. Holt & Co., New York, 1903), there are twenty eight such allusions in *The Merchant of Venice*, thirty in *Much Ado About Nothing*, while in *Macbeth* there are only eight and in *Othello* eleven. However, *Hamlet* is full of them, and *Antony and Cleopatra*, although the subject here perhaps has something to do with it, has more of them than any other great tragedy. The references to the more common or familiar myths or mythological figures are to be found in all his works. In the last plays allusions become abundant again. Whereas in his early period Shakespeare often uses mythology as a mere rhetorical device or an ornament, in his middle period his use of it becomes more functional. In comic situations he often resorts to mythology either to parody the antiquated style of tragedies which was crammed with allusions (as in the language of Pistol) or to create a comic effect by contrasting the seriousness of the allusion and the levity of the situation (as we find in some of Falstaff's speeches). Used more seriously, mythology serves as a kind of shorthand to create the feeling of beauty, passion or power above the ordinary level of mankind, or to give shape to the invisible powers of nature and bestow grandeur and dignity on natural phenomena. In the last plays, however, classical divinities have a more directly relevant function: they even appear in person sometimes, signifying providence and supernatural intervention (for example, Diana in *Pericles* and Jupiter in *Cymbeline*); or fertility and plenitude (as Ceres does in *The Tempest*); or they symbolise the power of regeneration, which is a theme of the plays (as in *The Winter's Tale*). A brief account of the world of Greek mythology on which Shakespeare draws is included here because of its relevance to his writings.

Although the English Renaissance is always described as classical, in the field of literature, and certainly in drama, it would be more accurate to call it Latin, since very few Greek poets, and not a single Greek tragedian, were translated into English in that period. The translation of Homer's *Iliad* by George Chapman did not start appearing until 1598, and was completed only in 1611, although the first ten books had been translated by Arthur Hall (in 1581), not from the Greek original, but from a French translation. Even Chapman used Latin aids in his translation. In the field of non-Homeric poetry only six idylls by the pastoral poet Theocritus were translated in 1588, and Marlowe began a poetic paraphrase of Musaeus's poem *Hero and Leander* (1593), which was completed by Chapman (in 1598). Greek drama was not available in English during the Elizabethan or the Jacobean periods (in fact, the first English translation of a Greek play, *Electra* by Euripides, appeared only as late as 1649), with the possible exception of one play by Euripides, *The Phoenissae*, a translation, or rather an adaptation, of which was made from the Italian in *Jocasta* by George Gascoigne in 1566. Nevertheless, largely through the medium of Latin, Greek myths and legends became widely known in England (as elsewhere), though often the gods and goddesses retained their Latin names. During the Renaissance authors throughout Europe made frequent use of handbooks and dictionaries of classical mythology: in England recent scholarship has shown that Spenser, Chapman and Ben Jonson used such handbooks. However, Shakespeare's knowledge of classical myths, as is seen from his use of them in his works, seems to be chiefly derived from the works of Ovid, the Latin poet of the first century B.C., and especially from his book *Metamorphoses*, which has been described as the source of nine-tenths of Shakespeare's classical mythology. Indeed few books have had a wider influence on later literature than the *Metamorphoses*.

In the *Metamorphoses* Ovid gathered together a large number of tales which have in common an element of transformation: tales of men changed into beasts, plants and stones. The book opens with the origins of the world, the change from chaos into the order and harmony of the universe. In what follows a brief account is given of the main incidents and figures of the world of Greek mythology which Shakespeare derived from Ovid, a knowledge of which seems useful for an understanding of his allusions. For further information consult E. I. Fripp, *Shakespeare Studies*, Oxford University Press, 1930.

In Ovid Shakespeare read how the god Saturn was dethroned by his strong sons, Jupiter, Neptune and Dis — although Shakespeare does not refer to Saturn as a mythological personage, that is, as the father of the gods, but as a planetary and astrological influence, namely as the source of the melancholy humour, or 'the melancholy god'. Jupiter or Jove was the mightiest of all the gods, and was sometimes identified by Shakespeare with the Christian God, or with the Hebrew Jehovah. He was the god of thunder and lightning, his wife was Juno, his herald Mercury and his page Ganymede. Shakespeare refers to all of these as well as to Jove's bird, the eagle, and his tree, the oak. In *Cymbeline* Jupiter appears on an eagle's back. Shakespeare also refers to the incidents in which, in order to satisfy his amorous desires, Jove assumed other shapes, like his changing into the shape of a bull to win Europa, daughter of king Agenor, and into the shape of a swan to get Leda. Neptune was the god of the sea, who appeared in Ovid and in Shakespeare's works with his arms, his sceptre (the trident) and his trumpeter Triton, who blew his hollow coiling trumpet to order the waves to be still. Dis or Pluto was the god of the underworld. In *The Tempest* he is called 'dusky Dis' and in *A Midsummer Night's Dream* 'king of shadows'. Shakespeare also refers to Dis's falling in love with Proserpina (Persephone, goddess of the spring), daughter of Ceres (Demeter, goddess of corn). While driving in his waggon on the surface of the earth Dis was shot by Cupid's arrows, and he fell in love with Proserpina whom he saw gathering flowers. Dis carried away the frightened young goddess and made her his queen in the underworld. There are many references in the plays to the underworld, the home of

Pluto, the land of Hades, Tartarus or the infernal regions; to three of its five rivers: Styx (the river of hate), Acheron (the river of grief) and Lethe (the river of oblivion); to Charon, the ferryman who wafted the souls of the departed to the underworld; to the three-headed hound Cerberus, which guarded the gates of Hell, the abode of Hecate, the goddess of sorcery and witchcraft; and to the Furies 'crowned with snakes' sent to torment the guilty and drive them into madness.

Among the other gods to whom Shakespeare makes continual reference is Apollo, the god of the sun, also alluded to as Phoebus, Hyperion, Titan and Sol. He is 'young Phoebus', and his outstanding characteristics are his golden hair ('Hyperion's curls') and his chariot with its wheels of gold and silver drawn by 'fiery-footed steeds'. Apollo's knowledge, his power of healing and his association with music are also mentioned. In *The Winter's Tale* Leontes sends to Apollo's temple at Delphi for an oracle. Because he was the god of medicine Ulysses refers to Sol's 'medicinable eye' in *Troilus and Cressida*, and recalling the picture of Apollo with a lyre Thersites calls him 'Fiddler Apollo'. The utter folly of Gertrude's choice when she preferred Claudius to her husband can be seen from Hamlet's words, when he likened his father to Hyperion and his uncle to a satyr — a lustful diety in human form with goat's ears, tail, legs and budding horns. The allusion is to the story of Midas, who was foolish enough to prefer the music of the satyr Pan to the immeasurably superior melodies of Apollo. To punish him for his stupidity and lack of discrimination Apollo changed his ears into those of an ass. Shakespeare also cites Apollo's love for Daphne. Apollo fell in love with Daphne at first sight and wanted to woo her; but she had decided to remain chaste like the goddess Diana. She ran away from him when he professed his love for her, and was pursued by him until her strength was spent, but in answer to her own prayers she was transformed into a tree, thus avoiding yielding to him. In four plays, *Henry VI Part 3*, *Two Gentlemen of Verona*, *Richard II* and *Romeo and Juliet*, Shakespeare alludes to the story of Phaeton, Apollo's son, who extracted a promise from his father to allow him to drive his chariot for one day, but he was unable to control the horses; the chariot ran out of its course and came so close to the earth that it nearly set it on fire. Jove, however, intervened to save the world and he struck Phaeton with a thunderclap.

Mercury (Hermes) was Jupiter's messenger. He wore winged sandals, and was noted for his swift and graceful movement. In Shakespeare's plays he also appears as the patron of crafty traders and of rogues (like Autolycus in *The Winter's Tale*). Like Apollo he was also a musician, although at the conclusion of *Love's Labour's Lost* we are told that the words of Mercury are harsh after the songs of Apollo. His musical powers were revealed when he cast sleep over Argus, before he killed him, an incident referred to in at least five plays. While making love to Io, Jove was surprised by his jealous wife, Juno; he therefore transformed Io into a cow. Suspicious of his behaviour, Juno asked him to give her the cow as a present. Juno then kept Io and ordered Argus to keep watch over her with his hundred eyes, two of which rested in turn. Taking pity on her suffering Jove ordered Mercury to slay Argus and release Io. Mercury assumed the guise of a shepherd, 'piped on oaten straws', enchanted Argus with his music, cast sleep on him with his magic rod, which induced slumber, and then cut off his head. His eyes, now their light was quenched, were taken by Juno and placed in the feathers of her own bird, the peacock, while to avenge herself on Io she made her wander in fear all over the world.

Of the goddesses that Shakespeare alludes to often Juno, sometimes referred to as Lucina (in *Pericles* and *Cymbeline*), was the most powerful. She was Jupiter's wife, described by Shakespeare as the 'Queen of the sky'. She was distinguished by her stately and majestic gait, to which Shakespeare refers in *Pericles* and *The Tempest*, and she drove in a chariot drawn by peacocks adorned with Argus's eyes. She was the goddess of marriage: in *The Tempest* she 'sings her blessings' on Ferdinand and Miranda. The god Hymen was her attendant and deputy at weddings, as we see in *As You Like It*. When Cleopatra thinks of herself as a wife, she swears by her (*Antony and Cleopatra* III xi 28; IV xv 24). Juno was known for her anger at Jupiter's infidelity and her merciless spite against her rivals: in *All's Well that Ends Well* she is described as 'despiteful Juno'. She was also the goddess of childbirth, her children were Vulcan and Hebe. To her Pericles prays when his wife is in labour. In *The Tempest* Iris appears before Juno and calls herself her messenger. Iris was the goddess of the rainbow.

Unlike Juno, Minerva or Pallas, the goddess of wisdom was a virgin. She was also the goddess of the arts, including the art of war. She was herself a warrior, pictured with a spear, helmet and aegis, a shield or breast-plate in which she wore Gorgon's head. The sight of this head was so terrible that anybody who looked at it was immediately turned into stone. In *Macbeth* Macduff likens the sight of the murdered Duncan to Gorgon's head. Arachne, who was a perfect weaver, was presumptuous enough to claim that Minerva's craft was not superior to her own, so Minerva punished her by breaking her flawless work and changing her into a spider.

Ceres was the goddess of agriculture. She was also the mother of Proserpina, whom Dis or Pluto kidnapped in his chariot and carried away to his kingdom in Hades. The distraught mother looked frantically for her lost daughter everywhere, until finally she found her in Hades. Jove responded to her entreaties and agreed to let Proserpina join her mother again for a period of six months each year. In the Masque in *The Tempest* she appears, attended by reapers, to take part in the celebrations held at the betrothal of Ferdinand and Miranda. However, she only agrees to come on condition that Venus will not be present, for it was Venus and her son Cupid who plotted Dis's kidnapping of Proserpina and Ceres could not forgive them that.

Venus was the goddess of physical beauty and desire. She was born in the Aegean sea on the shore of the island of Cythera, hence Shakespeare's calling her Cytherea in *The Winter's Tale* and *Cymbeline*. She drove to and from her home, at Paphos in Cyprus, in a chariot drawn by white swans or doves. In *The Tempest* Iris tells Ceres that she has seen Venus with her son, Cupid, on their way to Paphos 'dove-drawn'. Venus's husband was Jove's son, Vulcan, the god of fire and the smith's craft. He made the chariot of Apollo, the sun god, and his skill and artifice are alluded to by Shakespeare. Vulcan's black face is contrasted with Venus's fairness (in *Twelfth Night* and *Troilus and Cressida*). Venus, however, was unfaithful to him: she fell in love with Mars, the god of war (whose sister, Bellona, goddess of war, is also mentioned by Shakespeare in *Macbeth*). In *The Tempest* Shakespeare describes Venus as Mars's 'hot minion'. Venus's passionate nature was also revealed in her love for the beautiful youth, Adonis, whose attempts to reject her advances are treated by Ovid and by Shakespeare (in his poem *Venus and Adonis*).

Cupid was Venus's son, the result of her affair with Mars. That is why he is described in *As You Like It* as 'that same wicked bastard'. Cupid's blindness, recklessness and irresponsibility are referred to time and again in the plays. In *As You Like It* he is called 'that blind rascally boy'; in *Love's Labour's Lost* he is described as 'wayward' and 'wanton'; in *A Midsummer Night's Dream* as 'knavish lad'. He had wings which enabled him to fly anywhere and shoot his darts at anybody, human or divine. He had two kinds of arrows: one sharp with a point of gold to awaken love, and another blunt with a head of lead to quench it. In *A Midsummer Night's Dream* Hermia swears by 'Cupid's best arrow with the golden head'.

Another of the goddesses whose name recurs in the plays is Diana, goddess of the hunt. She was the exact opposite of Venus: she was a virgin goddess and stood for chastity and coldness. In *As You Like It* Orlando calls her the 'thrice crowned queen of the night' alluding to her threefold character: in the heavens she was the moon goddess, Luna, Phoebe or Cynthia; on earth she was Diana or Dictynna, the goddess of the hunt; while in the underworld she was the infernal deity, Hecate, goddess of witchcraft. On earth she went about accompanied by a band of nymphs, who after hunting bathed with her in her pool. She punished Actaeon, for daring to look at her while bathing, by turning him into a stag to be hounded by his own dogs.

Of the three sister Fates, the Parcae who wove the destinies of men and whose decrees even the gods could not alter, there is frequent mention in the plays. We hear of the 'Sisters Three' 'cutting' with 'shears' the thread of life in *A Midsummer Night's Dream, Richard II, The Merchant of Venice* and *Pericles*; in *Henry V* we find 'Parca's fatal web', in *As You Like It* the decrees of the Destinies and in *The Tempest* the Fates who 'stand fast'.

Among the other mythological material which Shakespeare derived from Ovid is the attempt made by the 'giants' to attack the kingdom of the gods and reach the stars by piling mountains one upon another, Pelion on top of Ossa, and Jove's retaliation by hurling his thunderbolt, smashing mount Olympus and flinging down the mountains Pelion and Ossa, thus crushing the giants. Hamlet refers to this incident in his angry speech to Laertes in the grave-yard scene. Shakespeare also refers to the story of the valiant hero Theseus, son of Aegeus king of Athens, in *Venus and Adonis* and in at least three plays. King Minos had waged war on

Aegeus and had twice given Athenian victims to the monster Minotaur, which was half bull, half man, and which he had shut away in an enclosure artfully designed by the famous and skilful artist Daedalus. When Theseus was taken prisoner and thrown in the maze, he was able to kill the Minotaur and trace his way back out of the labyrinth with the help of Minos's daughter, Ariadne, who was in love with him. He fled with her from Crete to the island of Dia, but he cruelly deserted her on its shore, where she stood all alone lamenting her fate. Because of Theseus's great fame the people of Calydon begged him to come to their aid and deliver them from the huge wild boar, which Diana had sent to them as a punishment for failing to make her any offering. He took part in the hunt for the 'Boar of Thessaly', the Caledonian Boar. He also fought the centaurs (the fabulous creatures, half men, half horses, which were given to lust and violence) and married Hippolyta, queen of the Amazons, the race of the female warriors. Their marriage, in fact, forms the central theme of *A Midsummer Night's Dream*.

Another story Shakespeare refers to is that of Tereus, Philomela and Procne. It is the story that Imogen was found reading before she went to sleep in *Cymbeline*. Tereus, who was married to Philomela, ravished his wife's sister, Procne. To make sure that she could not tell his wife what he had done, he had her imprisoned and cut off her tongue. Procne, however, was able to convey her story to her sister by means of a design which she had woven on a loom and which pictured what had befallen her. To avenge themselves on Tereus the two sisters killed Itys, the son of Tereus and Philomela, cooked his flesh and gave it to his father to eat. Procne was transformed into a swallow, Philomela into a nightingale, while Tereus was turned into a hoopoe. Equally violent was the revenge devised by Medea, one of the best known mythological figures. She was the daughter of the barbarian king Aeetes and she fell in love with the Greek hero Jason. Jason had led a party of Greeks to the palace of King Aeetes to ask for the golden fleece. By means of Medea's powerful magic he managed safely to fulfil her father's monstrous conditions. He took the gold back to Greece, accompanied by Medea whom he married. There to please him Medea, again by her magic, rejuvenated Jason's father, Aeson. Jason's affection for Medea did not last; he married a new wife, a thing that aroused Medea's jealousy and rage. Her revenge on him was violent and included her slaying her own and Jason's children.

Another tragic female figure was Niobe. Exulting in the fact that she had seven sons and seven daughters, Niobe considered herself superior to the gods. She was, therefore, punished by the angry gods for her pride and presumption; she lost all her children and her husband into the bargain, and was turned to stone by grief, swept by a violent whirlwind and set down on a mountain top with tears trickling from her marble face. Dido, the queen of Carthage, is also mentioned in the plays. She fell in love with the Trojan hero Aeneas and put an end to her own life when he deserted her. Perhaps the best known pathetic lovers were Pyramus and Thisbe. Their tale, though not of Greek origin, was told by Ovid. Shakespeare treats it humorously in *A Midsummer Night's Dream*. Pyramus and Thisbe, who were next door neighbours, were in love, but their parents forbade their marriage. They used to communicate through a chink in the wall between their two houses, and they finally decided to meet one night near a particular tree in the open country in order to run away. Thisbe was the first to be there, but seeing a lioness approaching she rushed quickly and hid herself in a cave, but unfortunately she dropped her veil. The lioness tore it to pieces and stained it with its bloodstained jaws, and then went away. A little while later Pyramus arrived, and noticing Thisbe's absence and the bloodstained shreds of her veil, he assumed that she had been devoured by a lion and killed himself with his sword. When she had recovered from her fears Thisbe came back to the tree only to see the body of her dead lover. She killed herself with Pyramus's sword.

No other single mythological figure, however, impressed Shakespeare so deeply, or left such a sure imprint on his imagination, as the semi-divine Hercules, 'the great Alcides', son of Jove and Alcmene. (Incidentally the sign of The Globe Theatre was Hercules carrying the world.) In his cradle Hercules crushed a snake, and when he grew up to be a man he accomplished many heroic deeds. Most of his twelve labours are mentioned by Shakespeare: for example, his slaying the Hydra, a monster with a hundred snake heads, two of which grew in place of every one cut off; his killing the huge Nemean lion; his dragging the terrifying dog Cerberus from the underworld; his relieving Atlas

whose duty was to carry the earth on his shoulders; his bringing
home of the apples guarded by the unsleeping dragon in the
garden of the Hesperides (the four sisters who guarded the
golden apples which Earth had given to Juno at her marriage to
Jove); and his slaying of Nessus, the centaur who tried to ravish
his beloved Deianira. Shakespeare also mentions Hercules's final
feat before his death, his swinging Lichas round three or four
times and his flinging him into the sea, sending his body soaring
into the sky. Lichas was the page who brought him from his wife
the fatal poisonous shirt that the dying Nessus had given her,
letting her believe that it was a charm for enkindling love.
Hearing a rumour that Hercules had fallen in love with another
woman, and hoping to reawaken her husband's love, she gave his
page Lichas the garment to give his master; but when the
unsuspecting Hercules put it on the poison seeped into his body,
and he met with his death. During his life Hercules's step-mother,
Juno, hated him, but after his death he became divine.

The largest number of classical allusions in Shakespeare's plays
comes from the story of the War of Troy. Part of this is treated in
Homer's epic *The Iliad* — the war broke out as a result of the
handsome Trojan prince Paris, son of Priam and Hecuba,
running away with Helen (Leda's daughter and symbol of beauty
and falsehood), wife of Menelaus, king of Sparta, and ended with
the victory of the Greeks and the burning of Troy. The story
provides the background of *Troilus and Cressida*. Although
Shakespeare read Chapman's translation of the first seven books
of *The Iliad*, from which he derived the character of Thersites, the
version of the story on which he relied was more medieval than
Homeric — a thing which shows to what extent the Renaissance
could still see classical antiquity through medieval eyes. The
source of nearly all medieval and Renaissance versions of the
Trojan war was not Homer, but the Latin authors Dictys and
Dares who lived in the fourth and sixth centuries A.D. respectively,
together with the parts dealing with Trojan matter in the works of
Virgil and Ovid.

In fact the story of the love of Troilus and Cressida was first
developed in the twelfth century, in the Old French *Romance of
Troy*, which became widely known through a Latin translation and
was later translated into English by Caxton as the *Recuyell of the
Historyes of Troye* (1475). The story had also been expanded by the

Italian author Boccaccio and subsequently treated by Chaucer and Henryson and Lydgate who dealt extensively with Trojan subjects in his *Troy Booke*. Shakespeare's sources in *Troilus and Cressida* seem to have been Caxton, Chaucer, Chapman's translation and probably Lydgate. Trojan characters appear again in *Hamlet* when Hamlet asks the player to recite Aeneas's tale to Dido, in which he tells her the story of Priam's slaughter and describes to her the sufferings of Priam's wife, Hecuba, whose lamentation and grief, in Shakespeare as in Ovid, moved the gods to pity. On the two occasions when Shakespeare deals with the subject it is clear that his sympathies lie with the Trojans rather than with the Greeks. This, however, is in keeping with medieval tradition: in the Middle Ages the nations of Europe claimed descent from the Trojan heroes. In fact, the story of the Trojan origin of Britain was generally accepted until the seventeenth century: it was believed that the country was called after Brutus, a descendant of Aeneas (the Trojan prince who founded Rome), who landed in Albion, where he ruled and was followed by a line of kings, among whom were Locrine, Lear and Gorboduc.

Shakespeare seems to have derived his knowledge of classical mythology from Ovid's *Metamorphoses*. Shakespeare certainly knew Arthur Golding's translation (1565–1567) which he echoes in certain places in his works and he must have known the *Metamorphoses* in Latin too. However, there are other sources from which he, like any other Elizabethan author who did not get a university education, must have derived, at least in part, his acquaintance with classical mythology. These can be divided into two classes, books and visual sources such as tapestry and pageantry.

Books which contained information on classical mythology were, of course, much more abundant and accessible in the sixteenth century than in the Middle Ages. Apart from Ovid (the most important of them all), there was much mythological information in the early English works about the Trojan war: Chaucer, Gower and Lydgate, who were widely read in the sixteenth century, as well as the more popular translation from the Old French romance by Caxton. In addition to books containing Trojan matter, about which at least ten literary works were written in the sixteenth century, there were numerous dictionaries and hand books of mythology in Latin throughout the sixteenth century, and a few in English such as: Stephen Batman's *Golden Booke of the Leaden Goddes* (1577); Abraham Fraunce's *Third Part of the Countesse of Pembroke's Ivychurch*, which contained sixteen tales from Ovid and Richard Linche's *Fountaine of Ancient Fiction* (1599).

However, the average reader did not need to read mythological handbooks to acquire a knowledge of classical myths. Mythology reached him indirectly through classical anecdotes and allusions he found in practically any book written in the sixteenth century. Because of the authority of the classics it was customary for authors to illustrate their books with such anecdotes and allusions; whether they were writing manuals of rhetoric, such as *Thomas Wilson* (1553) or creative works such as *A Mirror for Magistrates* (1563) and Lord Berve's *Golden Boke* (1534). Furthermore, many classical tales were treated in prose, for example, by Painter in *Palace of Pleasure* (1566–7) or by Greene in *Euphues* (1587) and *Penelope's Web* (1587). In short the Elizabethan reader could not avoid coming across mythological allusions in whatever he read.

It was, therefore, not surprising to find so many English Renaissance works, in verse and prose, with themes from classical mythology. Although the practice of versifying Ovid's tales was born in the Middle Ages, it received a fresh impetus in the sixteenth century. Classical mythology was treated even in ballads, and such ballads were especially abundant between 1560 and 1575 and must have helped considerably to spread the knowledge of the chief myths among those who could not read Ovid. There were ballads on the story of Pyramus and Thisbe (in 1566, reprinted in 1584); on Diana and Actaeon (1566); on Aeneas 'The Wandering Prince of Troy' (1564–5); on 'The lamentation of Hecuba and ye Ladies of Troye' (1586). Another genre which must have contributed much in this respect was the type of play with a classical or mythological subject, made fashionable by the University Wits (especially John Lyly), for example, George Peele's *The Arraignment of Paris* (printed in 1584), Lyly's *Campaspe* (1584) and *Galathea* (*c.* 1588) and Marlowe and Nashe's *Dido, Queen of Carthage* (printed in 1594). Between 1560 and 1600 at least one work dealing with mythology appeared every year, and in the last decade of the century four or five were published annually. For instance, the year 1595 witnessed the publication of the following:

R. B. (Richard Barnfield): *Orpheus, his journey to Hell and his music to the Ghosts.*
Richard Barnfield: *Cynthia, with certaine sonnets and the legend of Cassandra.*
George Chapman: *Ovid's banquet of sence.*
Michael Drayton: *Endymion and Phoebe.*
Thomas Edwards: *Ceaphalus and Procris; Narcissus.*
John Trussel: *The first Rape of Faire Hellen.*

And in 1596 appeared:

Dunstan Gale: *Pyramus and Thisbe.*
Peter Colse: *Penelope's complaint.*
W. Fiston: *The ancient historie of the destruction of Troy.*
Sir John Davies: *Orchestra.*
Edmund Spenser: *The Faerie Queene* (Bks I–VI).

The last two, although not chiefly about classical themes, contain a good deal of mythological lore. Spenser used mythology more extensively than any other English poet. Instead of calling natural phenomena by their real names, he almost always used the names of the classical divinities that stood for them: he used Phoebus for the sun and Diana for the moon. Almost all the outstanding Elizabethan poets wrote on subjects connected with classical mythology. Examples are George Gascoigne's *The complaints of Phylomena*, Robert Greene's *Planetomachia* (1585), *Euphues and Penelope's Web* (1587), Thomas Lodge's *Scillaes Metamorphosis* (1589), George Peele's *A Farewell and a Tale of Troy* (1589), Richard Barnfield's 'Hellen's Rape' (in *The Affectionate Shepherd*, 1594) and *Cynthia* (1595), John Marston's *The Metamorphosis of Pigmalion's Image* (1598), Henry Constable's *The Shepherds Song of Venus and Adonis* (1600), Thomas Middleton's *The Ghost of Lucrece* (1600), Francis Beaumont's *Salmasis and Hermaphroditus* (1602). There is no need to go further than the opening of the seventeenth century. What should be borne in mind is that Shakespeare's two mythological narrative poems, *Venus and Adonis* (1593) and *The Rape of Lucrece* (1594), are not just single solitary phenomena, but belong to a long tradition of poetry to be found not only in England, but also in Italy, France and Spain, a tradition to which they themselves contribute something. Middleton's poem *The Ghost of Lucrece* is a continuation of Shakespeare's, while *Venus and Adonis* did not lack imitators. Some of the characteristics of this type of poem are its richly decorative nature and its apparently sensuous or sensual quality, revealed in warm, detailed and colourful descriptions of the beauties of the female body. This lends some force to the belief that the Renaissance was distinguished by a recognition of the beauties of art, nature and the human body.

The Elizabethan reader and author did not derive their knowledge of classical mythology exclusively from literary works. There were other sources which account for the familiarity of the average Elizabethan with the chief mythological figures and made it possible for the Elizabethan theatre-goer to follow the allusions in Shakespeare's plays. Mythological stories were often depicted in tapestry and pageants. Ultimately the influence of Ovid could be traced here, an influence which could also be seen in Renaissance painting (of course, much more so on the continent than in England). A modern scholar once remarked that 'one cannot race too quickly through the Louvre or the Italian galleries to observe that Ovid rivalled, or excelled, the Bible as a storehouse of subjects'. This is indeed true, and helps explain why the modern average educated European is reasonably familiar with classical mythology. He need not study the work of the ancients or read dictionaries of mythology, but only needs to visit the chief art galleries or see reproductions of famous paintings of the Renaissance to acquire some knowledge of mythological figures. In the Induction to *The Taming of the Shrew* the Lord and his two servants, carrying on their game of pretence, ask the bewildered tinker, Christopher Sly, whom they want to deceive into believing he is a lord:

Second Servant: Dost thou love pictures? we will fetch thee
        straight
    Adonis painted by a running brook,
    And Cytherea all in sedges hid,
    Which seem to move and wanton with her breath,
    Even as the waving sedges play with wind.

Lord: We'll show thee Io as she was a maid,
  And how she was beguiled and surpris'd,
  As lively painted as the deed was done.
Third Servant: Or Daphne roaming through a thorny wood,
  Scratching her legs that one shall swear she bleeds;
  And at the sight shall sad Apollo weep,
  So workmanly the blood and tears are drawn.

(Induction ii 49 ff.)

In England tapestries, which were much more common than paintings, gave the ordinary man a chance to see classical myths represented in great pictorial detail. Whole stories, such as that of the siege of Troy, were sometimes depicted on 'painted cloth' hung on walls. For instance, Lucrece is described viewing such a painting (*Lucrece* 1 1366 ff.).

Equally important as an educational factor in this respect was the influence of pageantry. The Renaissance inherited the medieval passion for pageantry and, with the increase of classical knowledge, figures from classical myths began to take prominent parts in the designs of pageants. Already in 1503 Paris, Mercury and Greek goddesses appeared in a pageant held at Edinburgh to welcome the daughter of King Henry VII, although these rubbed shoulders with biblical characters, a curious example of the combination of Christianity and classicism which characterised the whole of English Renaissance to a much larger extent than the late Middle Ages. Under Elizabeth pageants, shows, processions and royal progresses became lavish and frequent. For instance, the famous entertainments offered to the Queen at Kenilworth Castle in 1575 included the representation of many mythological figures. Court masques, of which there is an example in *The Tempest*, were extremely popular, especially during the reign of James. They were a mixture of poetry, music, dance and rich costume, held loosely together in a way rather like the modern musical comedy, and they contained characters derived from classical history or mythology, such as Greeks and Trojans, nymphs and satyrs. Because of the popularity of such pageants practically every Londoner was expected to recognise the chief mythological figures, for example, Jove with his eagle, Juno with her peacock, Venus with her doves, Ceres with her sheaves, Fortune with her wheel and Hercules with his club and his lion's

skin. To realise how popular pageants, dealing with mythological
subjects, were in Shakespeare's time the reader may go to *The Two
Gentlemen of Verona* where he will find these words spoken by the
disguised Julia to Silvia:

> When all our pageants of delight were play'd,
> Our youth got me to play the woman's part . . .
> Madam, 'twas Ariadne passioning
> For Theseus's perjury and unjust flight.   (IV iv 157–68)

Another source of Shakespeare's classical knowledge, which deserves to be mentioned separately, is Sir Thomas North's translation of Plutarch's *Lives* (1579). This was not translated from its
original Greek, but from the French translation done by Jacques
Amyot. Plutarch was a Greek historian who lived between 50 and
120 A.D., and in this book he gives us vivid and subtle accounts of
the lives of famous Greek and Roman men who played decisive
roles in human history. The significance of North's translation is
not confined to its being one of the sources of Shakespeare's
knowledge of classical mythology; from it Shakespeare derived
his material for *Julius Caesar, Coriolanus, Antony and Cleopatra* and
in part *Timon of Athens*. At times he followed North's language
very closely indeed, as in his description of Cleopatra's barge in
Antony and Cleopatra (II ii 196 ff.), which the reader should compare with the account given by North to realise not only the extent
of Shakespeare's debt to his source but also how, with the
minimum of alteration, words can become great poetry. Furthermore, it has been claimed by a scholar (J. A. K. Thomson,
Shakespeare and the Classics, p. 250, George Allen & Unwin,
London, 1952) that through the medium of North's Plutarch
'Shakespeare divined the true spirit of Greek tragedy'. Whether
this is true or not is another matter and to consider it will lead us to
an irrelevant discussion of the full extent of Shakespeare's debt to
the classics, which is by no means our purpose here. Suffice it to
say, however, that Shakespeare's debt to Plutarch was very great
indeed.

Shakespeare seems to have been anxious in the beginning of his
career either to impress the world with his classical knowledge, or
to prove that he could tackle classical subjects and write in classical
forms; or perhaps as a young man he could not avoid taking for

his models the kind of writing that was admired by the educated at the time. His poems, *Venus and Adonis* and *The Rape of Lucrece*, both of which deal with classical subjects, belong to the tradition of mythological poetry which was fashionable in the Renaissance. His early comedy, *The Comedy of Errors* (1592–3), was based upon the *Amphitruo* and the *Menaechmi*, two plays translated freely from the Greek by the Roman playwright Plautus, whom Shakespeare seems to have read. In *Hamlet* when Polonius announces the coming of the Players the only two dramatists he mentions by name are Plautus and Seneca. The influence of Plautus on Shakespeare is not great: from him Shakespeare only borrows the plot of this one play, and we do not need to know Plautus to understand *The Comedy of Errors*, which is after all a very minor play. However, with Seneca the case is different: he exercised a great influence on the whole of Elizabethan tragedy, on its form no less than on its content. Seneca's influence on Shakespeare is very indirect, but no student of the dramatist can afford to ignore it. It is not simply that Shakespeare's early attempts at writing tragedy, *Titus Andronicus* and *Richard III*, show marked Senecan qualities. There are certain features of Shakespearean tragedy, even in its most mature form, which we can understand better when we know something about Seneca's plays.

Seneca was a Roman dramatist (and a philosopher) of the first century A.D., who wrote what has been described as 'chamber-drama' tragedies designed to be recited and not to be acted on a stage (see F. L. Lucas, *Seneca and Elizabethan Tragedy*, p. 56, Cambridge University Press, 1922). The fact that his plays were meant to be recited accounts for some of their characteristics. In the first place the emphasis in them is thrown on the language, which is violently rhetorical; they are full of colourful descriptions and artificial dialogue, especially what is known as stichomythia (studied dialogue in short alternate lines). Secondly, because the plays were not written to be acted on the stage they are full of horrors and bloody deeds, which are not generally reported by messengers as we find in Greek drama from which they are borrowed. For they are mostly taken from Greek plays, chiefly by Euripides, the last of the great Greek tragedians, whose plays deal with Greek myths or legends unusually full of horror and blood. These include: *The Mad Hercules, Trojan Women, Medea, Phaedra, Oedipus, Agamemnon* and *Thyestes*.

Like Ovid, Seneca was destined to exercise a great influence on the development of Western literature, an influence by no means proportionate to the intrinsic artistic value of his plays which are now considered to be almost worthless. Yet no Latin author was regarded as superior to Seneca in the Renaissance. In England the most enlightened critics like Webbe, Ascham, Puttenham and Sidney thought highly of his plays, which were taken by all, including Shakespeare apparently, to be the model of classical drama. Whenever the English Renaissance critics talked of the tragedy of the ancients it was Seneca and not Aeschylus, Sophocles or Euripides that they had in mind. This is less surprising when we remember that there were no English translations of Greek drama until the middle of the seventeenth century. Even those of the English poets and critics who could read Greek (and they were very few indeed) must have found the world of Greek tragedy more alien than Seneca's. The Christians could see a resemblance between their Pauline ethics and Seneca's ethics, both of which preach the need for the subjugation of passion by reason. In fact, Seneca himself was felt to be so Christian-like that some one forged a correspondence between him and St Paul.

Seneca's influence on English drama started very early. He was one of the few authors whose works were used as text books at school. His plays were often performed at the universities of Oxford and Cambridge in the original language (since scholars did not then realise that they were not meant to be acted) together with Latin imitations of them. The first of his plays to be translated into English appeared in 1559 and by 1566 seven plays had been translated. In 1581 the *Ten Tragedies* were collected and edited by Newton. The very first English tragedy proper, Sackville's *Gorboduc* (produced in 1561 and published in 1565) was heavily indebted to Seneca, and was praised by Sidney because its style rose to 'the height of Seneca's style'. *Gorboduc*, it is true, was the first of a long series of plays known as academic or classical tragedies, which were generally written by pedantic authors to satisfy the taste of a pedantic audience and their appeal was of course very limited. English popular drama developed along different lines but, however different from academic tragedy, it was by no means free from Senecan influences. For Seneca's influence came through indirect channels too: some of the contemporary French and Italian plays which the Elizabethans translated into English were themselves markedly Senecan in form and style, for instance, *Cornelia* and *Antonius* by the French author Garnier, the former translated by Kyd, the author of *The Spanish Tragedy*, the latter by the Countess of Pembroke, Sir Philip Sidney's sister. After their appearance in translation Seneca's plays were pillaged by popular dramatists. In a well-known passage in his Preface to Greene's *Menaphon* (1589) Thomas Nashe attacked those dramatists

> that feed on nought but the crumbs that fall from the translators' trenchers ... English Seneca read by candlelight yields many good sentences, as *Blood is a beggar*, and so forth, and if you entreat him fair in a frosty morning, he will afford you whole *Hamlets*, I should say handfuls of tragical speeches.

The reference to *Hamlet* is interesting, though of course Nashe is referring not to Shakespeare's *Hamlet*, but to an earlier play by the same name. The two Elizabethan authors in whose work the popular and the classical most noticeably meet are Kyd and Marlowe, two authors to whom Shakespeare is deeply indebted. Kyd is the supposed author of that earlier play on Hamlet generally taken to be the immediate source of Shakespeare's play, while the influence of Marlowe on Shakespeare is not confined to his 'mighty' line of verse or to his power of drawing characters on a superhuman scale.

Seneca's lasting influence on Shakespearean tragedy may be usefully studied under four headings: form, subject-matter, style and general philosophy. We must make it clear, however, that we are not trying here to assess Shakespeare's debt to Seneca; for that matter of all Elizabethan dramatists Shakespeare owes least to him. Shakespeare must have read at least some Seneca in the original, but his *direct* debt to him is negligible, compared with that of Marston or Chapman or even Ben Jonson. What should be emphasised is that certain features of Shakespeare's plays, which they share with the rest of Elizabethan drama, may cease to be puzzling when they are traced back to their ultimate Senecan origins.

To Seneca's example Elizabethan drama owes its five-act structure, although here the influence of the example of the Latin dramatist Terence too cannot be ignored. Nor can we ignore the importance of the authority of the Latin poet critic Horace, whose *Art of Poetry* was perhaps the most influential piece of ancient criticism from the Renaissance right down to the eighteenth century. In his *Art of Poetry* Horace notes the division into five acts as a rule to be observed, but it was largely Seneca's example that the dramatists imitated. Another formal feature of some of Seneca's plays, which is sometimes to be seen in Shakespeare, is the use of a messenger who reports some violent action that takes place off the stage (as the murder of Macduff's children in *Macbeth*). Although, unlike the Greeks, Seneca does not always observe stage decencies and in this respect he is followed, indeed excelled, by the Elizabethan dramatists. Seneca's example only helped to strengthen the practice of showing horrifying deeds on the stage, inherited from medieval miracle plays, where violent actions such as the slaying of the children or crucifixion take place within sight of the audience. In a play like *King Lear* the blinding of Gloucester takes place on the stage. Another formal characteristic of Shakespearean and Elizabethan tragedy in general, which is commonly ascribed to Seneca's influence, is the part played by the ghost and other supernatural agents, especially those of the underworld such as witches or furies. Although ghosts and furies were not unknown in Greek tragedy, in Seneca's plays they became a regular feature, and their part was considerably enlarged. For example, in *The Mad Hercules* there is a detailed description of the horrors of Tartarus, the ultimate descendants of which are Clarence's account of his dream before his death in *Richard III*, and the Ghost's description of his sufferings in *Hamlet*. Many of Seneca's plays (like Shakespeare's *Hamlet* later on) open with a ghost. *Thyestes* begins with the ghost of Tantalus, driven by a fury, and in *Agamemnon* the action begins with the appearance of the ghost of Thyestes. There is even a ghost in his *Oedipus*, the ghost of Laius. In *Medea* Medea and Atreus invoke the furies to help them in their revenge, much as in *Macbeth* Lady Macbeth invokes the powers of evil to come to her aid.

Seneca was able to use these ghosts and other supernatural paraphernalia because his tragedies deal chiefly with revenge. In this respect Seneca can be described as responsible for the birth of the Elizabethan Revenge Play, a long line of plays in which the theme of revenge takes 'the crude form of blood asking for blood', and whose greatest contribution to English drama was

Shakespeare's *Hamlet*. Seneca chose the most sensational subjects for his plays, which partly reflects the blunted sensibility of his age: murder, incest and slaughter of children. His sensationalism appealed to the Elizabethans who enjoyed scenes of violence, like bear-baiting and public executions. Together with revenge went the stock character of the cruel and scheming tyrant, although here the Senecan tyrant combines with the biblical figure of Herod in the Miracle plays (and the Renaissance image of the Machiavellian type of person) to produce the character of the typical tyrant in Elizabethan drama. An example of such a tyrant is Richard III, although Richard possesses other qualities too, which make him a much subtler figure than the usual Elizabethan stage tyrants. Still, he orders the murder not only of his own brother, but of the young princes, his nephews too. In *Titus Andronicus* and the three parts of *Henry VI* there is an abundance of physical horror. It is not that this is a quality of the early plays alone (although it must be admitted that in the later plays the impression that horror is pursued for its own sake is no longer given). In *Hamlet, Macbeth* and *King Lear* there are plenty of 'carnal, bloody and unnatural acts', but here violence is used by Shakespeare as an occasion for the unfolding of tragedy, for reflection and probing into the mystery of the human condition.

As for Seneca's influence on the style of Elizabethan drama it can be seen in two characteristics. First is its tendency towards exaggeration, artificiality, rant and bombast to accord with the scenes of violent passion of which the plays are full. There is no need to go to the earlier plays of Shakespeare for examples, although of all the Elizabethan dramatists Shakespeare suffers least from this defect. In the earlier plays, especially in *Titus Andronicus* and the three parts of *Henry VI* and even in *Richard III*, this inflated, declamatory and rhetorical style seems to be the norm. In the later and more mature plays it is used only sparingly and deliberately, and it is reserved for certain characters such as Hotspur in *Henry IV*, or certain scenes such as the grave scene in *Hamlet* where we find the altercation between Hamlet and Laertes. In some cases it is used, as in *Hamlet*, to distinguish the language of the main actors of a play from that of the characters in the play within play.

Secondly, Seneca's influence on the style can be seen in the use of elaborate descriptions, of what is disparagingly described as 'purple passages', of the strewing of the dialogue with moral maxims and 'sentences' and most of all in the use of stichomythia. Here is a famous example of stichomythia from *Richard III*:

> *Gloucester*: Lady, you know no rules of charity,
>   Which renders good for bad, blessings for curses.
> *Anne*: Villain, thou know'st no law of God nor man:
>   No beast so fierce but knows some touch of pity.
> *Gloucester*: But I know none, and therefore am no beast.
> *Anne*: O! wonderful, when devils tell the truth.
> *Gloucester*: More wonderful when angels are so angry.
>   Vouchsafe, divine perfection of a woman,
>   Of these supposed evils, to give me leave,
>   By circumstance, but to acquit myself.
> *Anne*: Vouchsafe, diffus'd infection of a man,
>   For these known evils, but to give me leave,
>   By circumstance, to curse thy cursed self.
> *Gloucester*: Fairer than tongue can name thee, let me have
>   Some patient leisure to excuse myself.
> *Anne*: Fouler than heart can think thee, thou canst make
>   No excuse current, but to hang thyself.
> *Gloucester*: By such despair I should accuse myself.
> *Anne*: And by despairing shouldst thou stand excus'd
>   For doing worthy vengeance on thyself,
>   Which didst unworthy slaughter upon others.
>
> (I ii 70–88)

Finally, Elizabethan tragedy, including Shakespeare's, was profoundly influenced by Seneca's philosophy as it is expressed in his plays. This is something different from the individual sentiments and reflections on general topics like beauty, fame, fortune, war, glory, country life, poverty and humility. (Elizabethan drama is full of such reflections, sometimes expressed in a form very close to Seneca's.) The influence meant is that of the general attitude to life (and to death) revealed in Seneca's plays. It is essentially an attitude of stoicism and of fatalism, of indifference to the vicissitudes and accidents of life, and of utter contempt for death. Seneca's characters, even the least courageous of them, either die by their own hands, or eagerly meet death. The same contempt for death, the same stoical fortitude, can be seen in the characters of Elizabethan drama, in villains no less than in heroes, and in men and women alike. Seneca's fatalism is most apparent in plays such as *King Lear*, while the way most of Shakespeare's characters resolutely choose to die or welcome death when it comes to them is strongly reminiscent of Seneca. The general indifference to the accidents of life, which was part of Seneca's stoicism, was incorporated in the general Christian and rational attitude of the Renaissance to life, discussed in the previous chapter. Here it is enough to give the example of Hamlet's account of Horatio's character, in which Horatio can be called both a good Christian and a 'Senecan man':

> For thou hast been
> As one, in suffering all, that suffers nothing,
> A man that fortune's buffets and rewards
> Has ta'en with equal thanks; and bless'd are those
> Whose blood and judgment are so well co-mingled
> That they are not a pipe for fortune's finger
> To sound what stop she please. Give me that man
> That is not passion's slave, and I will wear him
> In my heart's core, ay, in my heart of heart,
> As I do thee.   (*Hamlet* III ii 65–74)

This is another instance illustrating how the classical and the Christian traditions meet.

6 Elizabethan Stage Conditions

Although the first researches into the conditions under which Shakespeare worked were motivated more by antiquarian interest than by literary considerations, it is now universally realised that some knowledge of those conditions is indispensable for a fuller understanding of his plays. The student of Shakespeare should know something about the structure of the Elizabethan stage, about the manner in which the plays were acted and the general likes and predilections, reactions and expectations of the audience that attended their performance. Being a successful dramatist, Shakespeare had to take all those factors into consideration and they have helped in some measure to define the form of his plays.

THE THEATRE

English drama was by no means a new phenomenon suddenly born (or imported from Renaissance Italy) in the Elizabethan age. When Shakespeare began to write for the stage England had known an almost continuous tradition of acting, whether religious or secular, amateur or professional, lasting for more than two centuries. Miracle plays, interludes and moralities were still acted in the sixteenth century, together with the more developed type of secular drama, the precursor of Shakespeare's plays. These varieties of dramatic entertainment were presented on more than one type of stage. It is true that scholars write of the Elizabethan stage as if there was only one type, but this is done only for the sake of convenience, for in point of fact there were four kinds of theatre used in Shakespeare's time, and his plays were presented at some time or other in practically all of them. These were: (1) the hall stage at Court, the universities or in the mansions of the nobility; (2) the inn yard; (3) the open-air public theatre; and (4) the private theatre. They were all in some form or other influenced by the native medieval traditional mode of staging.

Medieval drama was not performed in a theatre, a building specially erected for the purpose. The mystery plays were shown in the open air in a market place, on a village green or at a street corner. The cycle of mystery plays were acted simultaneously in different parts of a village or a town; each play, or rather episode, in the cycle was performed on a raised platform, placed on wheels, called a 'pageant'. The pageant consisted of two floors; the lower was curtained all round and served as a dressing room and on the upper the actors appeared. They could descend from the upper floor by means of steps or ladder to the street where they sometimes also acted. When the performance of one episode was completed the pageant was drawn away to be replaced by another pageant on which the following episode was given. The pageant was fitted out with trap-doors and other devices to enable characters such as devils to disappear into a substage called 'hell'. Pageants seem to have been symbolically decorated. Painted flowers and trees represented Paradise while a dragon's head from which flames issued forth stood for Hell. Costume was used somewhat conventionally; for example, God appeared in ecclesiastical dress, devils in leather suits and angels were pro- vided with wings. Together with this generally conventional and symbolical mode of presentation went a certain crude type of realism, which could be seen especially in scenes of violence. For instance, blood spurted out of bladders in the scene representing the Massacre of the Innocents.

As for medieval secular drama, the farcical interlude, which was generally performed in the halls of the great and the rich, it was given on a raised dais or platform, curtained at the back, with no scenery but with quite a few stage properties like a throne, a chair, etc.. What is important to note in the medieval stage is the mixture of conventionalism and crude realism, the absence of scenery with the result that the stage was neutral and that it took its locality from the actors' words. We shall see that these features were substantially retained in the Elizabethan stage.

VARIETIES OF THE ELIZABETHAN STAGE

THE HALL STAGE

This was basically the same as the medieval dais: a raised platform at one end of the hall, be it a nobleman's hall or a college dining hall at the universities of Oxford and Cambridge, or at the London schools of law, the Inns of Court, which were regarded as the Third University in the Kingdom. The platform had a back curtain through which the actors could enter or leave the stage, otherwise they might use doors in the hall leading into other rooms. Hall-stage performances varied a great deal: at the royal court they were naturally very elaborate affairs and only less lavish than court performances were those given at the Inns of Court, whose students were generally older and richer than those at Oxford and Cambridge. However, both at the universities and at the court staging involved the use of various stage properties like caves, stocks and thrones and to some extent the use of scenery, that is, a number of *fixed* decorations on the stage, representing various objects: for instance, a palace, a castle, a city, etc.. The most striking feature of the court and university performances was, in fact, the marked tendency to use elaborate stage machinery like trap-doors and ingenious devices to produce a variety of sound and scene effects like thunder and lightning. In the course of time the spectacular element of these performances became dominant, and by the beginning of the seventeenth century not only the court but even an Oxford College (Christ's Church) enlisted the help of Inigo Jones 'the much travelled architect', to produce spectacular scenic effects. In such performances the influence of the contemporary Italian stage, with its heavy emphasis on ingenious and eleborate scenic effects, could be easily seen.

THE INN YARD

Performances given at court, at the universities or in the halls of the nobility were naturally private performances, whereas those given in inn yards were public. It is here that we find the real beginning of the Elizabethan public playhouse. Inn keepers encouraged the professional actors to perform at their inns because, besides sharing some of their profit, they realised that it would attract more customers. At first actors used inn yards for certain seasons, but in the course of time certain London inns were virtually turned into theatres.

The Elizabethan inn (of which one extant example is the New Inn at Gloucester) was built round a quadrangular yard, the doors of the guest rooms opened on an open gallery overlooking the yard and running along all four sides of it. Against one wall a movable stage consisting of a platform raised on trestles would be set up for the actors to perform on and at the back of the stage would be a curtain through which they would enter or leave unless there were doors leading into the inn. Guests and well-to-do spectators would watch the show from the gallery, while the poorer sort would stand in the yard.

THE PUBLIC THEATRE

The structure

In many ways the stage of the inn yard helped to define the structure of the public theatre, which is the most significant type of theatre for our purposes, since most of Shakespeare's plays were written to be performed in it. There is no absolute agreement among scholars on the exact details of the structure of the Elizabethan public theatre. However, the main features, which are more or less generally accepted, are given. They are based on four sets of evidence: (1) a contemporary drawing of one of these theatres, The Swan, made by a Dutch traveller, Johannes de Witt, who visited the theatre soon after it was built in 1595 (see p. viii); (2) a picture of a slightly later date found on the title page of a play called *Roxana* by William Alabaster, published in 1630; (3) contemporary documents like the contracts for the building of three theatres, found among a collection of papers belonging to Philip Henslowe, the first Englishman to make a fortune in the theatre business; finally (4) the stage directions in the plays themselves.

As is clear from the drawing in Visscher's view of London (1616) the outside shape of the theatre was octagonal. The inside was either octagonal or circular. In *Henry V* Shakespeare describes his theatre (The Globe) as 'This wooden O'. This round shape which was much more convenient as regards seating accomodation than the quadrangular inn yard, was borrowed from that of the bear-baiting ring. In fact, in the early theatre the stage was a movable platform because the building was designed to serve both as theatre and as bear-baiting or bull-baiting ring. The inside of the theatre was divided into two roughly equal parts: the stage and the auditorium. The stage, a large platform standing on trestles and oblong in shape, jutted almost into the middle of the circular yard. The rest of the yard which formed the auditorium, was called the 'pit'. Here the spectators ('the groundings') stood because it had no seats; so they surrounded the platform from three sides. The pit itself was surrounded by three tiers of galleries, the uppermost of which was roofed generally with thatch. Unlike the pit, the galleries were provided with benches. The pit was open to the sky, but the stage itself was covered by a canopy, resting on two posts which rose vertically from the floor of the stage. No front curtain separated the stage from the audience. At the back of it could be seen two or three doors. The side ones were used for the entry or exit of actors and they led to the 'tiring house', that is, the dressing-rooms. The middle door, which was much larger, was curtained off and behind the curtain (or 'arras' or 'traverse', as it was sometimes called) the prompter must have sat. Until quite recently it was believed that when the curtain was drawn it revealed a recess which served as inner stage when necessary, and that Shakespeare made full use of this inner stage: for example, in *Romeo and Juliet* it served as Juliet's tomb, it was used as Desdemona's bed chamber in *Othello* and as a cavern in *The Tempest*. However, the theory that there was an 'inner stage' in the Elizabethan theatre is now generally discredited.

Below the stage was a basement or cellar or what was known as 'hell' (cf. the medieval stage) into which actors disappeared by means of a trap door and from which voices could be heard. For instance, the voice of Hamlet's ghost could be heard from it and the witches in *Macbeth* would vanish into it. In *Antony and Cleopatra* (IV iii) music is heard from under the stage. Characters, especially creatures from the lower world, devils, furies, ghosts, apparitions, were lifted up and down by means of an elaborate and efficient machine. The appearance or disappearance of such characters was often accompanied by loud and startling noises such as thunder or loud music.

Above the back of the stage the first gallery continued and was used either as a private box called 'the Lord's room', which was the most coveted place in the whole of the theatre, or else as an upper stage which could serve as an upper story of a building, the battlements of a castle or a city wall. For instance, it was used as the balcony from which Juliet talks to Romeo. In fact, any scene for which the stage direction is 'above' would take place there.

Over the stage was a superstructure, called the 'heavens', which comprised the stage cover or 'shadow', a hut and a turret. In the hut were placed stage property and the stage-hands who were responsible for operating a crane to lower or raise property or supernatural characters such as gods or goddesses on to the stage. From the 'heavens' a god would appear or speak or descend (like Jupiter on an eagle's back in *Cymbeline*). From the hut cannons were fired, alarm bells were rung and thunder produced. From it also a trumpeter blew his instrument to announce the beginning of a performance. The turret supported the flag-pole and the flag (showing the sign of the theatre: in the case of The Globe it was Hercules) which continued to fly until the end of the performance.

Scenery, Property and Costume

Little or no scenery was used on the public stage, although wall hangings were employed, whether these were coverings of tapestry to provide the rich background of a chamber in a castle or palace or painted cloth to indicate the setting of a humbler dwelling. Indeed with the audience surrounding the main stage it was virtually impossible to use any changing scenery. The result was that, like the medieval stage, the Elizabethan public stage generally took its locality from the words of the speakers. The best known example is the opening of the second scene of *Twelfth Night*, where this bit of dialogue occurs:

> *Viola*: 'What country, friends, is this?'
> *Captain*: 'This is Illyria, Lady . . .'

Sometimes a board was displayed to the audience, indicating the name of a town, for instance 'Rome', written in large lettering, accompanied perhaps by a picture of a city gate. This board, of course, was a stage property and not a piece of scenery.

There was much stage property used on the Elizabethan stage which was simply carried or drawn on stage by attendant actors. Contemporary records show that the properties used by one theatre company included a cauldron, a dragon, a tomb, a rock, a tree of golden apples, heads of men and animals. By means of property the stage could be localised for a scene. For instance, a table, a couple of chairs and one or two vessels would make it a tavern, while a tree in a tub might suggest an orchard or a forest to the audience. The entry of two or three soldiers with their swords and bucklers would immediately render it into a battlefield.

In contrast to the poverty of the stage in scenery the costumes displayed on it were exceedingly rich and magnificent. Very large sums of money were spent on these costumes. For instance, a garment used by one company in 1591, a 'black velvet cloak with sleeves embroidered all with silver and gold' cost over twenty pounds, and that was at a time when a chicken, we are told, cost three pence (£ 1/80) and a sheep four shillings (£ 1/5). Many contemporary authors commented on the rich apparel of players, although we must remember that in real life people, especially gallants, spent fortunes on their dress. As in medieval productions the ordinary dress of the time was generally used, irrespective of the period in which the play was set, although there was apparently an attempt, crude as it was, to distinguish Romans and Eastern characters generally by the kind of dress they wore. A Roman (and Greek) soldier was given a breastplate and a short sword. Likewise, a Turkish or Eastern character wore a turban and carried a scimitar, which was not an Elizabethan weapon. Jews, like Shylock, wore their Jewish gaberdine. It also seems that, in some respects, costumes on the Elizabethan stage were conventional and symbolical. Allegorical figures and classical gods and goddesses like Jupiter, Juno or Iris must have worn special dress. The prologue wore a long, black cloak. Black and white were used symbolically: in fact tragedies were often played against a background of black drapery on the stage. Black was, as indeed it still is, a sign of mourning. When Hamlet first appears on the stage he is dressed in black—a thing which immediately sets him off from the gaily and colourfully attired courtiers. Black was also sometimes an indication of an evil character, just as white symbolised innocence and chastity and was worn by angels and good spirits. The clearest indication of the conventional nature of at least some of the Elizabethan costumes is that there was in use what was called 'the robe to go invisible in' which was presumably a conventional mantle accepted both by actors and audience. What the colour of that robe was, is not known, but here we have an example of a purely conventional dress which has no counterpart in real life, something analogous to the use of black on the Japanese stage to secure the same effect of invisibility. In *The Tempest* Ariel must have worn such a costume.

THE PRIVATE THEATRE

The use of the term 'private theatre' here is not accurate since performances given at this type of theatre were no more private than those given at the public theatres. In fact, the only differences between the two types are the following. (1) Only the stage and galleries in the public theatre were covered, while in the private theatre the whole building was roofed in. (2) Performances at the private theatre were therefore given by artificial light and not by daylight as in the public theatre. The stage was illuminated by means of candelabra hung over it. (3) The price of admission to the private theatre was higher with the result that its audience was more 'refined'. Whereas the price of admission into the public theatre ranged from one penny to one shilling, (£1/240 – £1/20), in the private theatres it ran from sixpence to half a crown (£1/40 – £1/8). (4) Because it catered for the taste of a more courtly audience, the private theatre resorted to more elaborate devices, especially as regards scenery. It was more open to the influence of the court Masque, an aristocratic entertainment, which was rapidly gaining favour towards the end of the sixteenth century and the beginning of the seventeenth, and in which the emphasis was heavily laid on spectacle and scenery. (5) In the beginning the private theatre was used by boy-actors, but in 1608 the company of which Shakespeare was a member, while keeping its public theatre, The Globe, acquired the lease of a private theatre, The Blackfriars, which afterwards became its winter quarters. In fact, at about that time the open-air public theatre was beginning to fall in esteem and cater increasingly for the taste of a lower class of audience and to give place to the private theatre.

Most of Shakespeare's plays were written for the public theatre, especially The Globe. However, in the plays he wrote after his company began to use The Blackfriars, there is a marked tendency towards scenic display, which is clearly shown, for instance, in the masque-like element in *The Tempest* or the spectacular sudden appearances of the god Jupiter on an eagle's back in *Cymbeline*.

ACTORS AND METHODS OF ACTING

There were two types of acting companies in Shakespeare's time: the Children's companies and the Men's companies. The former were formed of the choir boys of St Paul's or of the Royal Chapel. In the Elizabethan age acting was regarded as part of the education of the young at schools and universities. Originally the boys were trained to act plays at the court, but from 1576 they were giving public performances at The Blackfriars private theatre in London and for a number of years successfully competed with the Men's companies. Among the distinguished playwrights whose works were acted by these boys were Lyly, Ben Jonson and Marston. The literary standard of the performances given by the Men's companies improved, and better authors such as the University Wits, including Marlowe, Greene and Nashe, began writing for them, and their social standing went up. As a result they gradually ousted the boys from the profession of acting, while recruiting the best elements in them to do their singing for them and to take various parts, especially the parts of women, which were always played by boys and young men. (The first actress to appear on the English stage was after the Restoration in the latter part of the seventeenth century.)

As for the adult professional actors of the Elizabethan age, they were the descendants of the medieval entertainers, the jesters and epic singers kept by the nobility. Travelling actors were still classed among rogues and vagabonds and other types of master-less men unless they were the retainers of a nobleman who was responsible for them. This is why groups of actors were known as

the servants of such and such a nobleman, even though they had
ceased to be retainers in the strict sense and were becoming
independent craftsmen, plying their trade. For instance, the
company for which Shakespeare started work was called Lord
Strange's Men; he later joined The Lord Chamberlain's Men, who
when King James I patronised them became known as The King's
Men. Another company which was a serious rival to it was known
as The Admiral's Men; they, together with The Lord Chamberlain's Men, were the best known companies in Elizabethan
England. Bearing the name of a lord meant that these actors
were protected by him and were at his service when called upon to
perform at his hall, although most of the time they gave public
performances wherever their service could be hired.

At first these performances were given in the yards of various
inns. They would share their profits with the landlord. Actors
would establish themselves for certain seasons in certain inns, and
in the course of time some inns were practically turned into
playhouses. However, they soon met with the strong opposition
of the city authorities who were predominantly puritan and who
objected to these activities, on the grounds that they encouraged
immorality, kept apprentices away from work and increased the
danger of infection during periods of plague. As a result of these
criticisms and of the measures taken by the city authorities to
prevent performances within the city boundaries, actors decided
that their survival depended upon having a permanent home for
themselves outside the jurisdiction of the London magistrates.
Consequently in 1576 the first public theatre, called The Theatre,
was erected just outside the bounds of the city. Before long a
number of theatres sprang up and were soon to become a regular
feature of London life and one of the sights foreign visitors to
London came to see. In 1577 The Curtain was built, The Rose was
set up in 1587, The Swan in 1595, The Globe in 1598, The
Fortune in 1599, The Red Bull about 1605 and The Hope in
1613. These theatres were generally financed by enterprising
small capitalists who saw the possibilities of the theatre business in
London. The companies of actors rented these buildings for a
certain period of time during which they shared some of the
takings with their landlord. The rule was that the money collected
at the main entrance went to the actors while that paid by the
occupants of the gallery was divided between them and the

landlord. The company to which Shakespeare belonged was fortunate enough practically to own The Theatre and when they moved to The Globe in 1598 it became entirely their own. This apparently was a unique position and accounts in part for the prosperity of the company which was composed on a joint stock basis. It was no accident therefore that outstanding actors and dramatists were attracted to it and that James I singled it out for the honour he conferred upon it.

When Shakespeare joined the acting profession the position of the professional actor was not as despicable as it was sometimes made out to appear, especially by the puritan assailants of the theatre. The best piece of literary criticism the Elizabethan age produced, Sir Philip Sidney's *Apologie for Poetry*, contains a noble defence of drama, tragedy and comedy alike. Besides, the interest in acting was widespread among the nobility and in the seats of learning. The court encouraged it and even practised it in such entertainments as the masque and plays were in some form or other performed by the scholars of Oxford and Cambridge as well as by law students in the Inns of Court in London. In *Hamlet*, Polonius who is Lord Chamberlain tells us with some pride that he once acted in a play on Julius Caesar. Prince Hamlet's own interest in the stage is a true reflection of the general interest in acting among the nobility at the time. When Shakespeare came to London to try his fortune in the theatrical world the actors had already acquired a permanent home for themselves. This indeed was a momentous event in the history of drama, for until then the feeling of security and stability necessary for the full development of any art was lacking. It was exceedingly unlikely that great drama should appear while actors remained mere wandering or strolling players. It is part of Shakespeare's good fortune that he had not appeared on the scene even a decade or two earlier. Having a stable home for actors resulted not only in the production of great plays like Shakespeare's, but to it also can in part be attributed the appearance of great actors capable of interpreting the great roles those plays contained. Among the most famous of these actors were Edward Alleyn (of The Admiral's Men) who played the heroic parts in Marlowe's plays, and in Shakespeare's company Richard Burbage who acted the parts of Richard III and Hamlet, Othello and King Lear, and the great comic actor William Kempe. Far from being mere vagabonds, Elizabethan actors were accomplished artists of international repute. They toured not only in the provinces, but also displayed their art in Scandinavia, the Low Countries and especially in Germany where they won great praise and esteem.

The training that the Elizabethan actor received was both exacting and varied. He had to be skilled in a number of things beside acting and theatrical delivery, ranging from fencing and wrestling to singing, dancing and music, since all of these things were required at some time or other on the stage. Those on the continent of Europe who witnessed their performance testify to the versatility of the Elizabethan actors. It is true that the vigorous competition which existed then between them meant that, like the dramatists, actors were kept very busy, continually rehearsing new plays. The demand for new plays was so great that the average run of a play then, we are told, was no more than ten performances. If one company put on a successful play, a rival company would commission its playwright, or a freelance author if it did not have the use of its own, to provide it as soon as possible with a new play on a similar theme. The well known example is Shakespeare's *As You Like It*, which The Chamberlain's Men put on as a result of the great success which The Admiral's Men enjoyed with their *Robin Hood*, a play which gives a picture of forest life. Likewise, old plays were being revived and brought up to date. Consequently, compared with modern productions an Elizabethan play must have been much under-rehearsed and less polished. On the other hand, Elizabethan acting was much faster and more vigorous. Compared with modern English acting, the Elizabethan style of acting would perhaps appear as too emotionalistic, crude and rather uncivilised. Of course, actors then were also acrobats and the structure of the stage offered them great opportunities for easy movement, up and down as well as across the stage. To make up for the lack of scenery they offered the audience a colourful display of costume in rapid motion. Unlike a modern English audience, the Elizabethans were not used to slow productions with long pauses enforced by the need to change scenery. Besides, plays were generally performed in their entirety and not in the cut versions so often to be seen on the London stage in modern times.

The problem of lighting meant that the plays could not last much longer than two hours. Further, the audience (at the public theatres) included the illiterate, and although these people were not unaccustomed to hearing eloquence and rich language (at least in churches) they could not be expected to possess the intelligence and subtlety of mind necessary for the understanding of at least some of the speeches in Shakespeare's plays. It was, therefore, necessary that delivery should be fast and that actors should try to achieve their effects as boldly and as swiftly as possible.

The speed of the production would not be the only thing to strike a modern Englishman visiting an Elizabethan theatre. Equally strange to him would be the rhetorical declamation of Shakespeare's lines, together with the conventional gestures of the actors. Recent investigations in Elizabethan methods of acting have pointed out the importance of the study of rhetoric in the training of the actors. The art of rhetoric was of course an important element in formal education at the time and it was widely practised by public speakers, lawyers and churchmen. On the stage actors used a large number of stock gestures expressing basic emotions like anger, fear or despair. These gestures were largely conventional: they were tacitly accepted by audience and actors and their main function was to contribute to the emotional concentration which poetic drama requires. However, they were not unrelated to real life and they were not purely stylised as is sometimes the case with gestures, in for instance, Indonesian dancing. The gestures of the Elizabethan actors were rather either an exaggerated form or a compression of real life gestures. This means that while the Elizabethan method of acting Shakespeare did not preclude realism, it did not attempt to offer an exact copy of real life, as we sometimes find on the modern 'naturalistic' stage. For instance, to express anger an actor would bite his lip or roll his eyes, to express bashfulness he would lower his eyes, in the case of distress he would cross his arms and hang his head down and if the grief was excessive and if it turned into despair, he might throw himself on the ground, as Romeo does in Friar Lawrence's cell when he hears the news of his banishment. He might even 'swoon' like Othello. On the other hand, to express joy an actor might easily caper about the stage. This sort of behaviour would, of course, be unthinkable on the modern English stage, where generally actors are expected to behave in exactly the same way as they do in real life.

Part of the emotional nature of Elizabethan acting can be explained by the fact that, compared with modern Englishmen, the Elizabethans were generally noisier, less inhibited and much more self-expressive in their speech and action. But, even after making this allowance, it would be exceedingly difficult to imagine the adult people then, in their ordinary every day life, fainting or throwing themselves on the ground on hearing sad news. The truth of the matter is that the Elizabethan mode of acting was more conventional than naturalistic; it was not meant to be an exact copy of real life behaviour. The most striking example of the conventional use of gesture then was the intricate use of hands and fingers: both in oratory and in acting fingers were made to express, or echo the expression of, a variety of emotions like supplication, triumph, despair, admiration, disapproval and lamentation. (On this point see B. L. Joseph, *Elizabethan Acting*, Oxford University Press, 1951.) In fact, gestures seem to have constituted such a necessary accompaniment of speech that we find Titus in *Titus Andronicus* (V ii 17–18) complaining that he cannot express himself adequately now that his hand has been cut off:

> how can I grace my talk,
> Wanting a hand to give it action?

Together with these conventional gestures we notice much on the Elizabethan stage that has a similar effect to that of pageantry and ritual. There are a large number of processional entries: nearly all principal characters enter the stage attended, often in a procession of varying degrees of elaboration. Coronations and funeral processions are abundant. To the same category belong the dumb shows, although these are not frequent in Shakespeare, the scenes of miming and silent acting, such as what we find in, for instance, *Hamlet*. Such scenes would naturally be acted in an even more exaggerated form than the rest of the play in which they occur.

THE AUDIENCE

Elizabethan audiences naturally varied a great deal from private to public performances. At the court, in the halls of noblemen, at the Inns of Court and in the Universities the audience would consist almost exclusively of the educated. But this was not true of public performances and even here the audience of a public theatre must have been different from that of a private theatre. Shakespeare wrote practically for every type of audience and we know that some of his plays were performed at the court. However, since the bulk of his plays (including most of his mature ones) were written for the public playhouse, it would perhaps be best to concentrate on the audience of this type of theatre. In any case, with the exception of royalty and the most eminent among the nobility, every class of society would be represented in the audience of The Globe. Similarly every type of person, except of course the puritans, would be present there.

The audience of most of Shakespeare's plays would therefore include a few people from the nobility and the gentry, and many citizens of London, especially the notorious young apprentices who, according to the city authorities, were enticed by the theatre to abandon their work and who often broke into riots outside the theatre doors. Amongst the Elizabethan audience could also be found many visitors to London who were attracted by the theatres as some of the chief highlights of the city, and a good many people who belonged to the underworld of London, such as rogues, pickpockets and prostitutes, who went to the crowded theatre in search of easy victims. The audiences of Shakespeare were therefore a mixed crowd which cut across all sections of the community. Shakespeare catered for groundlings as well as for those who occupied expensive gallery seats.

Why, it may be asked, were the illiterate groundlings attracted to Shakespeare's plays? The answer to this question sheds some light on the universality of Shakespeare's art. Shakespeare's plays appeal to various levels of taste and intelligence at once. They contain many elements which even the illiterate could enjoy. There is much exciting action in them like battles, single combats, wrestling and duelling, street brawls, mob scenes, and scenes of violence in general. There is also in them much that would appeal to the primitive interest in the various manifestations of the supernatural, like ghosts and witches. Likewise, Shakespeare satisfied the craving in his audience for watching pageantry, pomp and ceremony and ritual, by providing many scenes of pageantry and ceremonial processions. The plays also contain fools or clowns, whose subtle relation to the rest of the dramatic action could be seen and felt by the more discerning type of spectator, but who provided the crude groundling with the clowning and dancing and acrobatics they could readily appreciate. Furthermore, there are the songs and music which practically every play contains, elements that could be separately enjoyed by the less discerning audience. In short, those of the groundlings who went to the theatre for mere entertainment found plenty of it in Shakespeare's plays.

The groundlings cracked nuts and drank ale in the theatre and riots occasionally broke out among them. Contemporary references to them indicate that they were smelly, rowdy and noisy and not much gifted with good taste. However, they must have listened to the dialogue, otherwise they would not have paid their pennies or they would have gone to the neighbouring bearbaiting ring instead. The groundlings seemed to have enjoyed slanging matches and clever puns no less than adroit swordsmanship or scenes of violence. They were interested in language, in high-sounding words, in rhetorical and persuasive speeches. The illiterate among them were trained to listen especially to eloquent sermons read to them in churches.

As for the educated section of the audience, the oral and rhetorical tradition had played an important part in their education. The study of rhetoric which constituted an essential part of a school syllabus had left its mark upon author and audience alike. Modern scholars such as Madeleine Doran and M. C. Bradbrook have studied the patterned speech and various intricate rhetorical devices which the audience expected and authors supplied in their plays. The art of conversation was consciously cultivated by courtiers who as a result were the target of many a dramatist's satirical attack. People were fond of collecting sentences, pithy moral statements from books and plays. Because the English language was still in a relatively fluid state people were excited by its possibilities and were still fascinated by what they could do with it. Hence the passion for coining new words, for puns and play on words, and the haunting obsession with figures of speech, reflected in the fashionable artificial style with its excessive use of figures of speech known as 'euphuism'.

The audience of Shakespeare, both the educated and the

illiterate, then had one thing in common: the lively interest in language which could be encountered in all sections of society. They were interested not only in what the actors did on the stage, but also in what they said and in the way they said it. In fact, it was the existence of such an audience with a lively interest in words and melodious speech, among other things, that made Shakespeare's poetry possible. Moreover, as Shakespeare's audience was such a mixed crowd, and was not confined to a small class of intellectuals, Shakespeare was saved from the arid intellectualism which characterises most of the modern 'highbrow' type of play which appeals to an educated audience. Much of the vigour and vitality of the plays would perhaps have been wanting if during the act of composition Shakespeare had lost sight of the mixed nature of his audience.

A PERFORMANCE AT THE GLOBE

To get a clear picture of Shakespeare's audience and stage conditions let us reconstruct what would happen at a typical performance in a public playhouse like The Globe.

The day the performance was to be given, a flag bearing the sign of the theatre would fly from a flagpole placed at the turret of the theatre in order to let the citizens of London know that a play was going to be presented that day. The time of the performance was the afternoon, because it was given by daylight; the show usually began at two or three o'clock. To announce that it was about to start a trumpeter standing in the 'hut' blew three blasts on his instrument. People rushed to the theatre, entering by the main door which was made deliberately narrow to allow only a single file of traffic. Tickets were not known as the doorkeeper held a box into which every spectator dropped a penny. (In the case of a new play the admission fee was raised to twopence [£1/120].) Having paid, the spectator would walk into the open yard or pit and remain there standing among the groundlings, if he did not wish to pay more. The groundlings were the spectators who watched the performance standing in the pit surrounding the stage on three sides. On the other hand, he was admitted into the roofed gallery upon payment of another penny (or more) to a man known as 'gatherer', stationed at the entrance to the gallery.

In the gallery seats were provided and indeed private compartments, boxes or rooms, the best of which were known as the 'Lord's room', 'orchestra' or 'gentleman's room', 'twelve penny room' or box, which was on the first tier of galleries nearest the stage. At times gallants were even allowed to sit on the two sides of the outer stage itself (if they were prepared to pay extra for it) thus displaying the expensive, latest fashion they wore. The capacity of the whole of The Globe, when full, was estimated at just over 2000 (the pit, when full, was estimated to hold 600) but the normal attendance must have been considerably less. (See J. C. Adams, *The Globe Playhouse*, pp. 87–8, Constable & Co., London, 1961.)

If the arras hangings covering the back wall of the front stage were black the audience would know that they were going to watch a tragedy. In the case of comedy the hangings would be gaily coloured tapestry with mythological figures depicted on it.

The performance usually (but not always) opened with a 'prologue' or 'chorus' (as in *Romeo and Juliet* and *Henry V*), a man, dressed in a long black cloak, who came forward politely on the stage to introduce the play and explain its theme, addressing the audience courteously and asking for their indulgence for any shortcomings it might have. Applause was expressed by clapping hands, as it is now still, but disapproval took the form of shouting noisily, of hissing and mewing like a cat. The theatre, on the whole, was a noisy place. Performances were interspersed with a good deal of music and singing (by the actors): for instance, the entry of royal characters was marked by a flourish of trumpets. Guns were fired often – in fact, The Globe was burned down in 1613 as a result of the thatched roof catching fire when a cannon was fired during a performance of Shakespeare's *Henry VIII*.

Because of the absence of front curtains the production was very fast with no long intervals, so that it lasted approximately two hours. At the end of the play the 'epilogue', who was one of the characters of the play, often stepped forward to thank the audience and to beg for applause. This was followed by a jig, a comic scene which was a mixture of song, dance and a rudimentary plot dealing with an obscene theme, and in which about three actors took part. The flag continued to fly above the theatre as long as the performance was in progress but was hauled down when the show was over.

CONCLUSION

What light does the study of Elizabethan stage conditions throw on Shakespeare's plays?

In the first place, the study of the structure of the Elizabethan stage (the public theatre) and of the methods of acting and of costume, shows that, though not lacking in realism, Shakespeare's drama is closer to conventional drama than to the modern naturalistic type of play, which is meant to be produced on what is called the 'picture-frame' stage. Even if the Elizabethan actors (and playwrights) had wanted to create a state of complete verisimilitude they would not have succeeded because they were surrounded by spectators on three sides (and indeed sometimes on all four sides). The plays were performed by daylight and there was no artificial scenery to create illusion. So there was no question of the Elizabethan audience mistaking what they saw for real life. Unlike the audience of a modern play who generally just sit and expect to be shown the whole thing, the former had to exercise their imagination and to respond creatively to what they saw and heard or else miss much of the plays. Shakespeare himself says that he appeals to 'the imaginary' forces of his audience. For instance, in broad daylight, on an empty stage, a watchman carrying a lantern would immediately suggest to the audience that the action was taking place in a street at night. What we get in Shakespeare's drama is something from which the conventional, symbolical and even ritualistic aspect is not entirely absent, something that has not lost touch with the poetic method. The mixture of realism and conventionalism can be seen not only in the costume and methods of acting, but also in the poetry of the plays. On occasions we find that the dialogue stops and the action of a play is frozen while a long artificial speech is being delivered. Such set speeches are rife in the plays, for example, Jaques' speech 'All the world's a stage' in *As You Like It* or Mercutio's on Queen Mab in *Romeo and Juliet*, both of which would be absurd in naturalistic plays.

Secondly, in the modern theatre the actors are separated from the audience by means of the curtained proscenium arch, and the separation is made almost complete by means of the footlights which illuminate the stage while the auditorium is darkened. The Elizabethan playhouse did not know this division, and this perhaps explains why drama still retained its original social function. Because the relationship between actors and audience was a close one certain conventions were more naturally and readily accepted. Soliloquies (speeches in which the character reveals to the audience his innermost thoughts) and asides (lines addressed by one character directly to the audience and not to other characters present on the stage) became possible in a fairly intimate atmosphere where the actor is surrounded by audience. Again, another convention like that of double disguise, in which a female character (impersonated by a boy actor) is disguised as a male, was much more easily appreciated in such an intimate atmosphere.

Thirdly, the absence of a front-curtain and of scenery meant that the stage was neutral in that it took its locality from the words of the actor. This feature has been taken by some critics to be a mark of a primitive type of stage craft and hence of playwriting. But, in fact, it resulted in a great deal of flexibility both in writing and in acting. It directly affected the structure of the plays and without it the rapid changes of scene, so frequent in Shakespeare's plays, and indeed dramatically functional in some of them, would have been impossible. Likewise, the use of bold contrast between successive scenes would not have been so effective if a pause had to intervene on account of the dropping of a curtain and the shifting of scenery. The absence of the curtain may also explain a number of technical features which characterise the Elizabethan drama. For instance, to mark the end of a scene Shakespeare often concludes a blank verse speech with a rhyming couplet. Likewise, great care is taken to remove dead bodies in the course of action.

Fourthly, perhaps the most significant fact that the study of Elizabethan stage conditions brings out forcibly is the great importance attached to the poetry of the plays, the words spoken by the actors. The stage takes its locality from the words the playwright gives to the actors; and the scenery and atmosphere have to be suggested or evoked by the poetry of the plays. For instance, on the naturalistic picture-frame stage the illusion of night can be easily produced by means of darkening the stage and by light effects generally, whereas on the stage in an Elizabethan public playhouse, even when the night scene was rendered symbolically, most of the effect of night was produced through the poetry given to the characters. This may be why Shakespeare's plays in which some or most of the action takes place at night (like *Macbeth* and *Hamlet*), abound in passages which are deliberately designed to create with superb effect the atmosphere of night. However, the great poetry the plays contain would not have been possible if Shakespeare's audience, high and low alike, had not possessed a lively interest in words and in melodious language.

Shakespeare's drama, then, is poetic drama in which words should have the prime consideration. This is an important fact, which unfortunately is only too easy to forget. For instance, in most of the nineteenth century productions of the plays, practically every single object alluded to in the dialogue and which was meant to be imagined by the audience was given an external existence on the stage. Extremely costly and elaborately realistic settings were provided. On one occasion, we are told that real rabbits were exhibited to help create the atmosphere of *A Midsummer Night's Dream*. We are also told that in a production of *Antony and Cleopatra* at the turn of this century fountains of real water with real goldfish were placed on the stage. This manner of producing Shakespeare has, however, by now virtually disappeared, thanks to the efforts of enlightened producers who have benefited from the researches of scholars in Elizabethan theatrical conditions. Such researches have established that Shakespearean drama is primarily poetic drama; that Shakespeare assumed his audience was not passive but alert and mentally vigilant; and that, as an artist, he might not have attained such greatness had he found a less favourable medium, had his stage been less flexible or his audience less imaginatively or poetically inclined.

7 The Chronology and Sources of the Plays

In the first edition of Shakespeare's collected plays, the First Folio of 1623, the plays were classified into three types or categories, Comedies, Histories and Tragedies, the three conventional Elizabethan divisions of drama. This order was subsequently followed in later editions. Under these headings plays were arranged irrespective of their date of composition. The book began with *The Tempest* and ended with *Cymbeline*. In fact, for a long time no attempt was made to establish the chronological order of the plays, for the interest in the development of Shakespeare's art (and of any art for that matter) was a relatively late phenomenon in the history of literary studies. The first attempt to work out the order of succession of the plays was made towards the end of the eighteenth century and ever since the question of dating the plays has been one of the major concerns of Shakespearean scholars. To fix the date of a play scholars rely upon two types of evidence, external and internal. The former includes records of the performances of a play or allusions to it in the contemporary literature or the date of its publication or references in the play itself to known historical events. Internal evidence, for instance, evidence based on the style of the play and its versification, is generally less trustworthy, because it is less objective, but is used to corroborate other evidence.

Because of the enormous difficulties posed by the task of dating the plays no chronological arrangement can be regarded as certain. However, in the following table the order followed is the one which was accepted by E. K. Chambers and upon the approximate truth of which there is a certain measure of agreement among scholars.

Date	Comedies	Histories	Tragedies
1590–1		Henry VI Part 2	
		Henry VI Part 3	

Date	Comedies	Histories	Tragedies
1591–2		Henry VI Part 1	
1592–3	The Comedy of Errors	Richard III	
1593–4	The Taming of the Shrew		Titus Andronicus
1594–5	The Two Gentlemen of Verona		
	Love's Labour's Lost		Romeo and Juliet
1595–6	A Midsummer Night's Dream	Richard II	
1596–7	The Merchant of	King John	
1597–8	Venice	Henry IV Part 1 Henry IV Part 2	
1598–9	Much ado About Nothing	Henry V	
1599–1600	As You Like It Twelfth Night		Julius Caesar
1600–1	Merry Wives of Windsor		Hamlet
1601–2			Troilus and Cressida
1602–3	All's Well That Ends Well		
1604–5	Measure for Measure		Othello
1605–6			King Lear Macbeth
1606–7			Antony and Cleopatra
1607–8			Coriolanus Timon of Athens
1608–9	Pericles		
1609–10	Cymbeline		
1610–11	The Winter's Tale		
1611–12	The Tempest		
1612–13		Henry VIII	

A glance at the above table will bring out one or two things. First, that Shakespeare seems to have passed through certain clearly defined stages in his development. For instance, the great tragedies seem to be concentrated in one period, during which Shakespeare did not write many comedies and the few he did write were distinguished by their dark or sombre atmosphere. On the other hand, it seems that the good history plays were written at the same time as the great comedies. Likewise, in the final years of his writing career, Shakespeare appears to have relinquished tragedy altogether and to have returned to the world of comedy. Because of these interesting features, in the last quarter of the nineteenth century Edward Dowden divided the dramatic career of Shakespeare into four main stages, which he called respectively: (1) 'The workshop' — which is the period of 'dramatic apprenticeship and experiment'; (2) 'In the world' — that is the period of later historical plays and the joyous comedies; (3) 'Out of the depths' — which is the period of the serious comedies and of the great tragedies; (4) 'On the heights' — the period of the 'romantic plays', which, he says, 'are at once grave and glad, serene and beautiful poems'.

This 'four period doctrine', as it came to be known, has been severely criticised by some modern critics, mainly because of the sentimentality of Dowden's treatment. But it is difficult to find any other theory to replace it. The picture of Shakespeare passing from apprenticeship to the world of history and mirthful comedy and from that moving on to the world of serious comedy and the great tragedies, from which he emerges in the last romances, is basically true. Roughly contemporary plays like *Henry VI* and *The Comedy of Errors* obviously belong to an early period of experiment and apprenticeship, and they show unmistakable signs of immaturity, while the lyricism of *Romeo and Juliet* has more in common with the sparkling world of the comedies than with the dark world of the great tragedies of *Macbeth* or *King Lear*. *Pericles, Cymbeline, The Winter's Tale* and *The Tempest* clearly form one group, which represents the final stage of the development of the poet dramatist.

Another thing that emerges from a consideration of the above table is the sheer bulk of Shakespeare's creative output. During an active career, stretching over a period of just over twenty years, he wrote no less than thirty seven plays, at an average of approximately two plays a year. When we recall that Shakespeare had to shoulder other burdens as well, like acting and sharing in the management of his company, we realise that he must have worked exceedingly hard.

As a dramatist Shakespeare was in a sense a tradesman, catering for the needs of the moment. The demand for new plays was so great (as a result of the very keen competition between theatrical companies) that dramatists had to work rapidly to increase the company's repertoire of plays and sometimes two or three (or even more) playwrights collaborated on a play. Often when a company put on a play that drew a large audience, a rival company would commission its dramatist to provide a play on a similar theme as quickly as possible. To add to a company's repertoire it was not unusual for authors to get hold of earlier plays by other writers and make a few alterations in them, adding a few topical allusions to make them look new.

Given these theatrical conditions we can understand one feature of Shakespeare's drama, namely the lack of originality in the stories on which the plays were based. Shakespeare was not alone in this. Unlike modern playwrights, most Elizabethan dramatists did not trouble to invent the stories of their own plays. Their attitude to plagiarism was different from that of modern writers. Nowadays, when an author borrows the plot of his play he has to acknowledge his debt. Not so with the Elizabethans who drew upon a common body of literature freely and without acknowledgement.

The stories of Shakespeare's plays came from a limited number of sources. They were derived either from the prose and verse romances (English and foreign) or from North's rendering of Plutarch's *Lives*, or from Holinshed's *Chronicles*. Occasionally Shakespeare reworked the theme of an older play. Each of these groups must now be considered in some detail, the object being to give an impression of Shakespeare's use of his sources, and not in any way to attempt an exhaustive account of the sources of the plays.

The romances, which were tales of love and adventure, were very popular reading in Shakespeare's time. Not all of them were English; in fact, there were a few collections of translated tales, from Italian, Spanish or French. The works which were best known and made most use of were Italian, Boccaccio's *Decameron* (*c.* 1350), Cinthio's *Hecatommithi* (1565) and Bandello's *Novelle* (1554). Tales translated from these works were to be found in such collections as William Painter's *Palace of Pleasure* (1566), Barnabie Riche's *Farewell to Military Profession* (1581) and George Whetstone's *Heptameron of Civil Discourses* (1582).

The romances furnished Shakespeare with most of the stories

of the early comedies. In the very earliest of his comedies, when Shakespeare was still a beginner in the dramatic art, he derived the stories for his plots not so much from the Italian novella as from Roman comedy. In *The Comedy of Errors*, and *The Taming of the Shrew*, he relied on Plautus and Terence: the plot of the former play is derived from Plautus's *Menaechmi* or *The Twins* and *Amphitruo*, while the latter is indebted to the *Supposes* (1566), Gascoigne's translation of a play by the Italian dramatist Ariosto (which was in part an adaptation from Plautus and Terence). It is as if at this stage Shakespeare could not as yet see the dramatic possibilities of the romances, but felt safer in going straight to the Roman drama for his source.

With *The Two Gentlemen of Verona* begins Shakespeare's dramatic use of the romance material. Here the source is a translation of a Spanich romance, *Diana Enamorada*, by de Montemayor (published in 1582). In the romances Shakespeare found the framework of his early comedies. Love is a common theme in these plays and the romances provided him with his pairs of lovers involved in intricate situations and complicated adventures, with such conventions as girls disguised as boys and with the pastoral setting against which the actions take place. To love and pastoral life Shakespeare only added the comic themes. Needless to say, the whole thing was anglicised, so to speak: for the lovers, the simple pastoral life and especially the humorous characters, all strike one as essentially Elizabethan. *The Merchant of Venice, Much Ado About Nothing* and *Twelfth Night*—all owe in varying degrees a debt to Italian romances. *As You Like It*, too, is in many respects a dramatisation of a pastoral romance, *Rosalynde* (1590) by Thomas Lodge. Unlike his comedies, Shakespeare's tragedies do not as a rule derive their plots from the world of romance. Apart from the early tragedy *Romeo and Juliet*, which, as we have already said, has much more in common with the world of the comedies than with that of the later tragedies, *Othello* is the only tragedy which is based chiefly on romance. The direct source of *Romeo and Juliet* is the narrative poem *The Tragical History of Romeus and Juliet* (1582) by Arthur Brooke, which is ultimately derived from Bandello's *Novelle* (1554), while the source of *Othello* is Giraldi Cinthio's *Hecatommithi* (1565). In the last plays Shakespeare turned to romance once more. The world of the last plays with its pastoral setting, its idealised love, its improbable adventures, its conventions of lost children miraculously found and girls disguised as boys, is essentially the world of romantic fiction. *Cymbeline* owes much to Boccaccio's *Decameron* (*c.* 1350) and in *The Winter's Tale* Shakespeare's chief debt is to a pastoral romance by Robert Greene, called *Pandosto: The Triumph of Time* (1588).

The story of Shakespeare's dealing with romance material seems in fact to follow an interesting pattern. He went to the romances in his early period when he was writing in a comic vein and, after practically abandoning them in his tragic period, he returned to them while writing his last plays. One or two reasons for this may be suggested. First in the comedies, especially the early comedies, there is on the whole a happy atmosphere of love and joy. It was therefore natural that for his stories he should go to the romances, since the romances were tales of love and adventure with a generally happy outcome. Secondly, because the romances were stories of intricate situations Shakespeare resorted to them during those periods in his dramatic career when he was interested in situation rather than character. When he was most interested in character — as he was in the tragic period — he searched elsewhere for his plots. It is not without significance that the only mature tragedy based on romance, *Othello*, is chiefly a domestic tragedy of intrigue.

Before turning to the tragic period we must say a word about the English history plays. These were mainly derived from Raphael Holinshed's *Chronicles of England, Scotland and Ireland* (second and fuller edition, 1587) and Edward Hall's *The Two Noble and Illustre Families of Lancaster and York* (1547). Both Holinshed and Hall furnish most of the historical material of *Henry VI Parts 1, 2 and 3*, *Richard III* and *Henry VIII*. (Shakespeare is also indebted to Holinshed for *Macbeth, King Lear* and to some extent *Cymbeline*.) In the history plays Shakespeare did not slavishly follow his source, and his treatment of Holinshed was in a sense just as free as his treatment of the romances: he often felt the need to compress, omit, add to his material or rearrange the order of events. Generally he went to his source to obtain a framework for his plays, although he did not hesitate to follow the chronicle pretty closely if it happened to serve his purpose. In *Richard III*, for instance, practically all the details of the death of Lord Hastings come from Holinshed (or rather from Sir Thomas More who is Holinshed's unacknowledged source). But on the whole he chose from his material only those events which revealed motive and character. In his handling of his material for *Henry IV* and *Henry V* we notice quite clearly the development of his interest in character.

The character stage in Shakespeare also happens to be his tragic stage: and indeed the relation is more than mere coincidence, for after all character assumes a larger importance in tragedy than in comedy or even in historical drama. When Shakespeare began to be interested in character he first turned for his material to Sir Thomas North's translation of Plutarch's great work *The Lives of the Noble Grecians and Romans* (1579) which has already been discussed in another part of this book (see p. 88). The *Lives* themselves contain a series of lively character portraits and it is interesting to note that from this work Shakespeare derived the material of his first major tragedy, *Julius Caesar*, which contains his first serious attempt at delineating a truly tragic character. It also furnished him with the material of his other Roman tragedies, *Antony and Cleopatra* and *Coriolanus*, as well as with part of the material of *Timon of Athens*. Shakespeare did not refrain at times from following Plutarch very closely in the rich words of North's translation.

During this period in which he produced his most subtle character portraiture, Shakespeare also resorted to Holinshed's *Chronicle* — but this time with a difference. The story of *Macbeth* is derived from the *Chronicle*, but if you compare the way in which Shakespeare used the *Chronicle* in *Macbeth* with his handling of it in an early play like *Richard III*, you will realise the significant development of Shakespeare's dramatic powers. In *Richard III*, as in the other history plays on the whole, and despite the liberties he granted himself, Shakespeare followed history fairly faithfully, but in *Macbeth* history becomes subservient to character. In *Macbeth* character and the exigencies of character become the prime consideration. *Richard III* is basically a chronicle play, whereas *Macbeth* is a tragedy. Indeed, if we go to Holinshed we shall find the source of some of the details in Shakespeare's *Macbeth*. For instance, the dialogue between Ross and an Old Man in Act II, Scene iv, in which they discuss the various manifestations of disorder in nature accompanying the sacrilegious murder of King Duncan seems to come straight from Holinshed (see pp. 51–3). The resemblance to the original here may seem as close

as that between the details of the death of Lord Hastings in
Richard III and the account given in Holinshed. In fact there is an
important difference between the two instances. The details
borrowed in *Macbeth* do not come from Holinshed's history of
Macbeth or Duncan, but from his account of the murder of King
Duff (who was the great grandfather of Duncan) by Donwald. In
Macbeth Shakespeare was obviously freer in the treatment of his
material. He found a detail in Holinshed which, irrelevant as it
was historically to the death of Duncan, he did not hesitate to use
because he saw that it could serve his dramatic purpose. Similarly,
in the actual murder of Duncan Shakespeare by no means
followed Holinshed's history. Holinshed dismisses the murder
very briefly, but in the play the murder of Duncan could not have
been accomplished so simply. Shakespeare had to use it as a
crucial scene for the sake of the dramatic exigencies of his tragic
character. Also, to make it more effective he altered the age of
Duncan, who was historically a young man; just as in his portrayal
of Macbeth he brought in the details from the murder of King
Duff, which seemed to him to have greater tragic possibilities.
From a single sentence in Holinshed he developed the whole
character of Lady Macbeth:

> 'but specially [Macbeth's] wife lay sore upon him to attempt the
> thing, as she that was very ambitious burning in unquenchable
> desire to bear the name of a queen.'

Here too he fuses her with Donwald's wife. It is this greater
freedom in handling his material, this ability to seize upon
anything that could serve his dramatic purpose however unhis-
torical it might be, that makes the play a tragedy and not a history
play.

Besides seeking his sources in North's Plutarch and in
Holinshed's *Chronicle*, Shakespeare in this period reworked the
themes of already existing plays. It is now pretty certain that
before his *Hamlet* there existed a play, now lost, by the same
name — which was written by Thomas Kyd, the author of *The
Spanish Tragedy*. This play is often referred to as the *Ur-Hamlet*,
that is, the original *Hamlet*. Another of the great tragedies which
was written on the theme of a contemporary play, this time extant,
is *King Lear*, the main source of which is an anonymous play called

The True Chronicle History of King Leir And His Three Daughters.

After the period of tragedies Shakespeare returned to the romances for his sources. Generally in the last plays Shakespeare seems to have lost interest in individualised character and to be more drawn to idealised types and less probable situations. Moreover, the predominant theme of these plays is that of regeneration and reconciliation, which, however, are brought about after much suffering. Yet the evil in human existence, though by no means minced by the poet, is transcended in a kind of mystical vision which finds more harmony than strife and discord in the universe. It is, therefore, fitting for the poet to return to the world of love and wonder which the romances provided. For the atmosphere of the last plays is on the whole one of joy, it only differs from that of the early bright comedies in that the joy is more spiritual since it is the joy, not of innocence, but of a vision of life that has 'supped full with [tragic] horrors', but has also gone beyond tragedy.

Appendix
A Note on the Histories

Shakespeare's history plays, much more than his comedies and tragedies, tend to present certain difficulties to the student. Therefore a few remarks explaining something of the background issues they involve are included here.

The Elizabethan history play, or as it was then called, the chronicle play, is a kind of drama which was of an entirely English origin. Basically it is a dramatisation of a national historical event or a series of events. Unlike the comedy and tragedy which seemed to follow certain recognisable patterns, the history play tended to be episodic in structure; it harkened back to the miracle plays which related the lives of saints in such a way that one incident followed another for no reason other than mere succession in time. The chronicle play therefore often gives the impression of being formless. Because of the lack of models in this type of writing the chronicle play, especially in the hands of Shakespeare, sometimes attempted to follow the pattern of tragedy (for example, *Richard III*) while at other times it leant heavily on the side of comedy (*Henry IV, Part 1*). Besides, an early device to impose some shape on the unwieldy mass of historical material was for the chronicle play to adopt the pattern of a morality play where two opposite forces of good and evil battle for the soul of man: in the chronicle play the soul of man is represented by the King and by implication the State of England. A clear example of this structure is provided in *Henry VI, Part 2*.

No less than ten of Shakespeare's plays are classified as histories by the editors of the First Folio. They are the plays which deal with relatively recent events from English history: *King John, Richard II, Henry IV, Parts 1 and 2, Henry V, Henry VI, Parts 1, 2 and 3, Richard III* and *Henry VIII*. Shakespeare was by no means the only dramatist to write about the history of England, for in the Elizabethan period, the 'chronicle play' enjoyed great popularity. It is estimated that between 1588, the year the Spanish Armada

126

was defeated, and 1603, when Queen Elizabeth died, about 200 plays dealing with themes from English history were produced.

Why did the Elizabethan audience demand history plays? It has been suggested that the Elizabethan interest in English history was a manifestation of the people's belief in their national glory. Of course, there was much patriotic exultation in the Elizabethan days and we can see it seeping into serious works like Spenser's epic *The Faerie Queene*. However patriotism can only go part of the way towards explaining the Elizabethans' interest in plays dealing with their own history. Absolute patriotism and the sense of national glory may account for certain things in *Henry V* and even in *Henry VI, Part 1,* such as jingoism, or the clearly unsympathetic treatment of Joan of Arc. But nobody can claim that plays like *King John*, or *Henry VI, Parts 1 and 2* were merely attempts to satisfy patriotic feeling. The Elizabethans, in fact, were concerned about the future of their country. The Wars of the Roses (1455–1485) did not seem to them such ancient history as they do now. Nor was civil war a thing of the distant past. Shakespeare, as one scholar once reminded us, was six years old when the great rebellion broke out in the North of England in a desperate attempt to replace Queen Elizabeth by her sister, the Catholic Mary Stuart. In *King John* the Bastard says:

> This England never did, nor never shall,
> Lie at the proud feet of a conqueror,
> But when it first did help to wound itself.
>
> (V vii 112–14)

The same sentiment is expressed in the anonymous chronicle play, *The Troublesome Reign of King John* (printed in 1591). It was this concern about the future of England that gave the English history plays their peculiar urgency at the time. There was much anxiety lest England should make a wrong choice in the question of appointing a successor to Elizabeth. The interest in English history then was not only a manifestation of patriotic feeling, but also part of a vital concern about national survival. The Elizabethan preoccupation with politics was no less keen than that of twentieth century man. For many Elizabethans fear of Catholicism was no less, if not more real and oppressive than fear of communism or totalitarianism or colonialism or neo-colonialism in certain quarters today. This perhaps explains why it is only in the past few decades that Shakespeare's history plays have received the attention of critics on such a wide scale. Amongst other things Shakespeare's history plays showed the Elizabethans, in a dramatic form, the forces that went to the making and preservation, or caused the destruction, of a nation. That is why one critic maintained that the real hero of Shakespeare's history plays is not so much Henry IV or Richard II as England the Respublica itself. In this respect Shakespeare was still writing within the English dramatic tradition. For instance, in an early Tudor play, perhaps the earliest English chronicle play, *King Johan* (written by John Bale), which is a mixture of a morality and a history play, we get historical and allegorical characters side by side and amongst the allegorical figures is that of 'England' which appears as a 'widow'.

What was the Elizabethan view of history which Shakespeare wove into his history plays? In the middle ages history was largely a collection of records, centred on the church. The centre of the medieval world was religion and it was therefore natural that the main theme of history then was, as Tillyard says 'the revolt of the angels, the creation of man, the incarnation, the redemption of man and the Last Judgment'. Any human history was conceived only in relation to that theological scheme, which gave pattern to it and which lay behind the moralising comments on the fall of princes and the mutability of fortune. The Renaissance, on the other hand, dealt more with human history proper; it also brought in a more practical attitude to it. It is true that Sir Walter Raleigh attempted to write a history of the world which began with creation, but like a typical Renaissance historian he went on to treat things more mundane and more applicable to people's lives. The historian would select certain events of the past and interpret them in such a way that they would help towards understanding and controlling contemporary events. (The choice of such events from national history may be due to the growing self-consciousness of the nation as a nation in the Renaissance which lay behind the increasing interest in recording and treasuring national events, and in giving embodiment to the memories of national figures to ensure national survival.)

Although it introduced or rather intensified interest in human history, the Renaissance did not lose sight of the relation between human events and divine Providence. The immediate theme of

Shakespeare's history plays may be disorder in the form of civil war in England and continual defeat in France, but that disorder is at the same time seen as an aspect of a larger order in the universe. There is a wider religious setting against which human actions take place, for God has His own reasons for the occurrence of this disorder. He uses it as a means by which He reveals His divine plan. That is why to an Elizabethan audience Shakespeare's history plays had a religious and cosmic significance. In this connection it is interesting to see the Elizabethan attitude to a revolutionary modernist like the Italian political philosopher Machiavelli (1469–1527). Machiavelli maintained that politics are essentially secular, that political order or disorder are essentially matters of technique of ruling which have no relation to religion. For him politics did not have the philosophical or rather the religious significance they had for the Elizabethans, but are only secular matters whose aim is purely practical and related to the question: How can the ruler keep control and the unruly subjects be effectively controlled? Machiavelli believed that to secure this end any means was legitimate. It was largely because he omitted the presence of God in politics and denied His hand in operating man's actions, that to the Elizabethans the name Machiavel came to mean an intriguer and an unscrupulous atheist.

The religious significance of history which is implied in Shakespeare's history plays can best be studied under the following headings:

COSMIC ORDER

The Elizabethans believed that the whole of the universe presented an integrated pattern, that all created things were linked together and arranged in a fixed order based upon the principle of hierarchy. The details of this system of the universe are included in the chapter on Cosmology and Religion (see p. 48 ff.) but the main points are mentioned again here as a reminder. First, for harmony to prevail in the universe all things must keep to their appointed station in the total scheme. Secondly, the universe presents a significant pattern of correspondences; for instance, the oak to the plants bears the same relation as the dolphin to the fishes or the lion to the beasts. Thirdly, there is a sympathetic relation between the various planes of being, so that any disturbance on one plane would be echoed or would have its reverberation on the rest.

POLITICAL ORDER

The cosmic order is also reflected in the political order. We can hardly find a clearer exposition of the relation between the two than in the opening of a contemporary widely known homily called *'An exhortation concerning Good Order and Obedience to Rulers and Magistrates'* (first published 1547).

Almighty God hath created and appointed all things in heaven, earth, and waters, in a most excellent and perfect order. In heaven he hath appointed distinct and several orders and states of archangels and angels. In earth he hath assigned and appointed kings, princes, with other governors under them, in all good and necessary order. The water above is kept, and raineth down in due time and season. The sun, moon, stars, rainbow, thunder, lightning, clouds and all birds of the air, do keep their order. The earth, trees, seeds, plants, herbs, corn, grass, and all manner of beasts, keep themselves in order: all the parts of the whole year, as winter, summer, months, nights and days, continue in their order: all kinds of fishes in the sea, rivers, and waters, with all fountains, springs, yea the seas themselves, keep their comely course and order: and man himself also hath all his parts both within and without, as soul, heart, mind, memory, understanding, reason, speech, with all and singular corporal members of his body, in a profitable, necessary, and pleasant order: every degree of people in their vocation, calling, and office, hath appointed to them their duty and order: some are in high degree, some in low, some kings and princes, some inferiors and subjects, priests and laymen, masters and servants, fathers and children, husbands and wives, rich and poor; and every one have need of other; so that in all things is to be lauded and praised the goodly order of God, without the which no house, no city, no commonwealth can continue and endure or last. For where there is no right order, there reigneth all abuse, carnal liberty, enormity, sin and

babylonical confusion. Take away kings, princes, rulers, magistrates, judges and such states of God's order, no man shall ride
or go by the high way unrobbed, no man shall sleep in his own
house or bed unkilled, no man shall keep his wife, children, and
possessions in quietness, all things shall be common; and there
must needs follow all mischief and utter destruction both of
souls, bodies, goods, and commonwealths.

This passage is particularly interesting because it occurs in a homily
which was read to the people throughout the reign of Queen
Elizabeth. Both as a child and as a grown man, Shakespeare must
have heard it in church. The ideas expressed here on the close
link between the cosmic and political order formed therefore an
integral part of the religious and civic education of the common
man. The *Book of Homilies* from which the above extract is derived,
was officially placed in churches by the Elizabethan Church, and
intended to be read aloud to the congregation on Sundays, as an
effort to promote conformity of doctrine amongst all. It is not
surprising then to find these commonplaces in Shakespeare's
history plays, where the parallel between political and social order
and natural order (as is exemplified for instance in the bee
kingdom in *Henry V* I ii) is constantly drawn.

THE POSITION OF THE MONARCH

Among men, therefore, the king enjoys the same status as the oak
among the trees, the eagle among the birds, the lion among the
animals or the sun among the heavenly bodies. The king rules by
undisputed divine right. He should therefore be obeyed because
to rebel against him is to rebel against God. This belief is crucial to
the understanding of the pattern of Shakespeare's history plays.
For a clear and unequivocal statement of it we may go to the same
homily, that reservoir of the political commonplaces of the time:
there we find, backed by suitable quotations from the Bible, the
following principles. (1) The king has a divine right to rule: 'as it is
written of God in the book of the Proverbs, *Through me kings do
reign* ... Here let us mark well, and remember, that the high
power and authority of kings, with their making of laws,
judgments and offices are the ordinances, not of man, but of God'.

(2) The king must always be obeyed, for: 'St Paul threateneth no less pain than *everlasting damnation to all disobedient persons*, to all resisters against this general and common authority, for as much as they resist not man, but God'. (3) If, however, the king's orders conflict with God's commandments then disobedience is allowed, but then it must be passive disobedience. Subjects should not resist but be content with suffering patiently. (4) Under no circumstances then are subjects allowed to show violence to the king, even when he is wicked. 'Christ taught us plainly, that even the wicked rulers have their power and authority from God: and therefore it is not lawful for their subjects to withstand them, although they abuse their power.' Subjects are 'not to withstand their liege lord and king; not to take a sword by their private authority against their king'. (5) 'Traitors and rebellious persons bring upon their own heads the terrible punishment of Almighty God.' The evil consequences of any rebellion are greater than the evil it was meant to redress.

This exaggerated religious aura which kingship had acquired by Shakespeare's time was in fact the product of deliberate Tudor propaganda, designed to discourage further rebellion and civil war. Coming after the Wars of the Roses Henry Tudor felt rather uneasy about his title to the throne, and to strengthen his position he sought first to encourage the notion of the divine right of kings, secondly to propagate through his historians a particular view of English history according to which the union of the two houses of York and Lancaster through his marriage with the York heiress was regarded as the inevitable and divinely ordained happy ending to the melancholy events of the preceding period. Another factor contributing to the increase of reverence for the figure of the king was that after the breach with Rome the English Church began to view kingship with a flattering eye. Besides, in the hearts of the people the void created by the removal of the figure of the Pope was later partially filled by the king.

In Shakespeare's plays in general, and not only in his histories, the religious significance of kingship is only too apparent. Readers of *Macbeth*, to choose an obvious example, are struck by the profundity and abundance of its religious imagery, of which this comment on the murder of King Duncan may serve as an example:

> Most sacrilegious murder hath broke ope
> The Lord's anointed temple, and stole thence
> The life o'th' building.(II iii 66–8)

The history plays are full of references to the divine sanction of kingship. Nevertheless, in Shakespeare's history plays we do not find the extreme principle of absolute obedience to an evil monarch. Armed resistance against Richard III (and against Macbeth) is clearly sympathetically portrayed, although it may be argued that neither king lawfully succeeded to the throne. Shakespeare was clearly aware of the existence of the tragic implication of the situation when two cogent rights conflict: obedience to the king and obedience to the dictates of one's conscience. For instance in *Richard II* we have such a situation where John of Gaunt stands powerless, unable to avenge the death of his own brother, in spite of the entreaties of his wife, the Duchess of Gloucester, because it is the king who was responsible for his death, or, as he put it:

> God's the quarrel; for God's substitute,
> His deputy anointed in his sight,
> Hath caus'd his death; the which if wrongfully,
> Let heaven revenge, for I may never lift
> An angry arm against his minister   (I ii 37–41)

Gaunt's words are clearly in accordance with the teachings of the homilies.

Because of this divine sanction of monarchy which meant that to the king the subjects owed absolute obedience and allegiance, the king's responsibility towards his subjects was felt and believed to be truly great. Shakespeare's history plays are full of references to the heavy burden of responsibility laid upon the shoulders of the monarch. To discharge his duties to his subjects properly and to see to it that order should prevail in the state, to prevent chaos and disorder from ravaging the state in the form of rebellion and civil wars, the king had to be a good and efficient ruler. He had to possess the right personality, and that meant that he had to possess certain traditional virtues, like courage, cunning, and justice or disinterestedness, symbolised respectively by the lion, the fox and the pelican. Because so much depended on the strength of the monarch's character, the subject occupied the attention of Shakespeare when he was interested in the theme of man in his political setting. His plays provide studies in kingly character: in some ways *King John* is a study of a weak monarch while in *Henry V* we are given the study of a strong king.

THE DIVINE PATTERN OF HISTORY

Likewise, in Shakespeare's history plays is embodied the Tudor view of recent English history as expressed in the main sources of the plays, especially Hall's *Chronicle*. This view states that the recent events leading up to the accession of Henry Tudor were closely linked together by a moral chain of cause and effect and that the whole thing followed a divine plan. Briefly the details of this divine plan are as follows: the trouble started with the quarrel between Henry Bolingbroke and Mowbray, which Richard II was unable to resolve and which resulted in the deposition of Richard. For that, and for his even more serious breaking of his faith in allowing the sacrilegious murder of Richard to take place, God punished Henry (IV) of Lancaster by making his reign full of internal troubles. However, God's full punishment was postponed in the reign of his son Henry V, because of his piety and his attempt to expiate his father's sin by having Richard reburied in Westminster. Unlike Richard II, Henry V was a good and strong king, but God chose to make his life short and His punishment was realised in the reign of his weak son, Henry VI, who was only a child when his father died, a thing which was a bad omen in itself. His reign was marked by internal strife (incessant quarrelling and intriguing among the nobles) and by external defeat abroad (whatever his father had won in the wars in France was forfeited by him). The result was the weakening of the house of Lancaster and the emergence of the descendant of the house of York, Richard, Duke of York, as claimant to the throne. Hence the Wars of the Roses, which occupy *Henry VI, Parts 2 and 3,* and in which many atrocities and butcheries were committed and complete anarchy and disorder reigned. This was symbolised by Shakespeare in a scene in which, unwittingly, a father kills his son and a son his father. At first victory fell to the house of Lancaster but later the Yorkist Edward (later Edward IV) returned and resumed the fighting swearing that he only sought his dukedom of York, not the throne, but he did not keep his oath. Eventually he won the war, but because he was a good king God postponed His punishment for perjury till after his death. (His brother, Gloucester — later Richard III — caused his sons to be murdered.) Richard III committed many sins, including the murder of King Henry VI in the Tower, he was therefore punished by his defeat at the hand of Henry Tudor (later Henry VII) who was clearly God's minister in delivering England at last from her long and dark night of misery and in bringing order out of disorder. The feud between the two houses was healed by his marriage to the heiress of the house of York. But the glory that was to be England was attained only in the reign of the issue of the two houses, Henry VIII.

Two things emerge from this account: first, evil and wickedness never pass unpunished, but each sin brings about the punishment it deserves. Secondly, Divine Providence ordained that events should be such that they would culminate in the 'triumphant reign' of the Tudors.

When we turn to Shakespeare's ten history plays we find that, apart from the two dealing with the reigns of the first and last English kings, namely *King John* and *Henry VIII*, the plays form two groups, each consisting of four closely linked plays. The first group or tetralogy, in the order of writing, contains the three parts of *Henry VI* and *Richard III*. In the second there are *Richard II*, the two parts of *Henry IV* and *Henry V*. In both groups of plays this pattern of English history is clearly revealed. The deposition and murder of Richard II is referred to time and again as a heinous sin which eventually unleashed the forces of disorder that were only vanquished by the intervention of Divine Providence through the person of Henry VII. In both Shakespeare dramatises the whole period of recent English history covered by Hall's *Chronicle*, beginning with the inception of the trouble during the reign of Richard II and ending with its resolution by the victory of Henry Tudor.

The ideas discussed above form only the political and intellectual background of the history plays. However, it would be a mistake to assume that Shakespeare wrote his plays to expound these ideas or that his aim was to preach to his contemporaries the folly and dangers of civil war or to provide effective propaganda for the Tudor regime. We cannot even prove that he personally believed in the Tudor view of the War of the Roses. In his histories Shakespeare was primarily a dramatist whose chief concern was to create enjoyable works of art. And it is as works of art that the plays ought to be approached and not as historical documents embodying the political commonplaces of the Elizabethan age — even though these commonplaces have to be grasped by the reader in order that he may have a clearer view of the situations in which characters in Shakespeare's plays are placed and have to make significant choices. As a serious artist Shakespeare used the political thought of his time, but only as the raw material of the plays. To read the histories with a view to defining and tracing the political thinking of the time is no less ludicrous than to go to Milton's *Paradise Lost* for the ptolemaic cosmogony it embodies. For in Shakespeare's history plays the apparent theme may be English history and English kings, but the real one is definitely human nature: man in his relation to the state; the fascinating variety of human behaviour revealed by the exigencies of public life; the attraction of authority and conflict of powers; the marriage or divorce between politics and morality; the sufferings of individual human beings when caught in the grip of clashing national events. These are eternal themes which are not confined to a particular time and place. Not long ago we saw some of them treated in the moving Russian novel, *Dr Zhivago* (by Pasternak). This point should be emphasised because there is a danger, implicit in the historical approach, of regarding the plays as period pieces or historical curiosities.

Index